THEMATIC UNIT
DINOSAURS

Written by Diann Culver

Illustrated by Sue Fullam

Teacher Created Materials, Inc.
6421 Industry Way
Westminster, CA 92683
www.teachercreated.com
©1993 Teacher Created Materials, Inc.
Reprinted, 2000
Made in U.S.A.
ISBN-1-55734-238-5

Table of Contents

Introduction

Dinosaurs contains a captivating whole language, thematic unit. Its 80 pages are filled with a wide variety of lesson ideas and reproducible pages designed for use with intermediate children. At its core are two high quality children's literature selections. For each of these books, activities are included which set the stage for reading, encourage the enjoyment of the book, and extend the concepts gained. In addition, the theme is connected to the curriculum with activities in language arts (including writing suggestions), math, science, social studies, reading, and art. Many of these activities encourage cooperative learning. Suggestions and patterns for bulletin boards and unit management tools are additional time savers for the busy teacher. Furthermore, directions for a student-created Big Book and culminating activities, allowing students to synthesize their knowledge in order to produce products that can be shared beyond the classroom, highlight this very complete teacher resource.

This thematic unit includes:

- ❑ **literature selections**—summaries of two children's books with related lessons (complete with reproducible pages) that cross the curriculum

- ❑ **poetry**—suggested selections and lessons enabling students to write and publish their own works

- ❑ **planning guides**—suggestions for sequencing lessons each day of the unit

- ❑ **writing ideas**—daily suggestions as well as writing activities across the curriculum, including Big Books

- ❑ **bulletin board ideas**—suggestions and plans for student-created and/or interactive bulletin boards

- ❑ **homework suggestions**—extending the unit into the child's home

- ❑ **curriculum connections**—in language arts, math, science, social studies, reading and art

- ❑ **group projects**—to foster cooperative learning

- ❑ **a culminating activity**—which requires students to synthesize their learning to produce a product or engage in an activity that can be shared with others

- ❑ **a bibliography**—suggesting additional literature and nonfiction books on the theme

---

To keep this valuable resource intact, so that it can be used year after year, you may wish to punch holes in the pages and store them in a three-ring-binder.

Introduction *(cont.)*

Why Whole Language?

A whole language approach involves children in using all modes of communication: reading, writing, listening, observing, illustrating, experiencing, and doing. Communication skills are interconnected and integrated into lessons that emphasize the whole of language rather than isolating its parts. The lessons revolve around selected literature. Reading is not taught as a separate subject from writing and spelling. For example, a child reads, writes (spelling appropriately for his or her level), speaks, listens, etc. in response to literary experiences introduced by the teacher. In this way, language skills grow naturally, stimulated by involvement and interest in the topic at hand.

Why Thematic Planning?

One very useful tool for implementing an integrated whole language program is thematic planning. By choosing a theme with correlative literature selections for a unit of study, a teacher can plan activities throughout the day that lead to a cohesive, in-depth study of the topic. Students will be practicing and applying their skills in meaningful contexts. Consequently, they will tend to learn and retain more. Both teachers and students will be freed from a day that is broken into unrelated segments of isolated drill and practice.

Why Cooperative Learning?

Besides academic skills and content, students need to learn social skills. No longer can this area of development be taken for granted. Students must learn to work cooperatively in groups in order to function well in modern society. Group activities should be a regular part of school life and teachers should consciously include social objectives as well as academic objectives in their planning. For example, a group working together to write a report may need to select a leader. The teacher should make clear to the students and monitor the qualities of good leader-follower group interaction just as he or she would state and monitor the academic goals of the project.

Why Big Books?

An excellent cooperative, whole language activity is the production of Big Books. Groups of students, or the whole class, can apply their language skills, content knowledge, and creativity to produce a Big Book that can become a part of the classroom library to read and reread. These books make excellent culminating projects for sharing beyond the classroom with parents, librarians, other classes, etc. Big Books can be produced in many ways and this thematic unit book includes directions for at least one method you may choose.

Digging Up Dinosaurs

by Aliki

Summary

Digging Up Dinosaurs is one of many books, written by Aliki Brandenberg on the subject of dinosaurs. It is from the popular collection of "Read-and-Find-Out-Books" from Harper and Row Publishers.

Digging Up Dinosaurs explains the slow, methodological process of fossil hunting. Each step is described in detail as paleontologists carefully remove the fossil from stone, prepare it for transport, and ship it to a museum. The book explains how scientists put the fossilized bones back together to make a complete dinosaur skeleton for display in the museum. The illustrations in the book are interesting and pictures of the dinosaur fossils are very detailed.

The outline below is a suggested plan for using the various activities that are presented in this unit. You should adapt these ideas to fit your own classroom situation.

Sample Plan

Day I

- Introduce the book. Use the ideas on page 6 as pre-reading activities.
- Read pages 1–8.
- Introduce the dinosaur bulletin board (page 34), Dinosaur Egg-citement, and related activities (pages 6–8).
- Introduce Dino-Dictionary Skills (page 9) and make a Dinosaur Folder (page 19).
- Do Magnitude Measures (page 13) and Creature Features (page 16).

Day II

- Read pages 9–24.
- Do Dinosaur Hunters see pg. 18 activities (page 18).
- Rotate through Fossils: File Folder Learning Centers (pages 19–26).

Day III

- Read pages 25–32.
- Do Dinosaur Classification (pages 27).
- Complete Dinosaur Venn Diagram. (page 28)
- Choose a dinosaur for Dinosaurs Report (page 29).

Day IV

- Research and write first draft of Dinosaur Report.
- Create fact/opinion web from "Are There Living Dinosaurs?" (page 30.)

Day V

- Read other books written by Aliki. (See bibliography.)
- Choose a book and write to the author.
- Write final copy of Dinosaur Report. Make cover and title page.
- Make Dinosaur Food. (page 7)

Overview of Activities

SETTING THE STAGE

1. Set the mood with an interactive **Dinosaur Bulletin Board.** Directions are given on page 34. Hang posters, mobiles, and dinosaur cutouts in the classroom. Use the Fingertip Facts information and picture cards (pages 60–77) with the bulletin board.

2. **Dinosaur Egg-citement:** Make a papier mache "dinosaur egg" filled with treats to hatch at the end of the unit. (See page 8 for directions.)

3. **Dino-Dictionary Skills:** Make a Dinosaur Folder for writing activities and vocabulary development. Introduce the Pronunciation Guide (page 9) that will be used throughout the unit. Direct the students to keep the pronunciation guide and a list of unfamiliar words in the folder for reference when writing.

4. **Digging into Picture Books:** Use the ideas on page 10 with this book, as well as other picture books, to help intermediate age children focus on particular ideas or concepts about fossils and dinosaurs.

ENJOYING THE BOOK

1. **Section by Section:** It is recommended that the book be divided into short segments for better understanding of the concepts. A summary of segments and discussion information is given on pages 11–12.

2. **Magnitude Measures:** Brainstorm about dinosaur size. Elicit predictions about height, length, and weight. Write the predictions on the chalkboard or a chart. Direct students to complete the math problems on page 13 and then use the answers to graph and compare dinosaur height and length on pages 14–15. Assign students to small groups to make large graphs comparing dinosaur and elephant weights. (See page 13.) Finally compare student predictions with the graphs.

3. **Creature Features:** Use the Mesozoic Plant and Animal Pictures from Fingertip Facts to develop descriptive writing with step-by-step student directions on page 16 and Creature Feature Words on page 17.

4. **Dinosaur Hunters:** Dinosaur hunting began in 1822 when huge teeth were discovered in England. Since that time thousands of dinosaur fossils have been recovered. Experience the process of recovering and reassembling dinosaur fossils using pages 18–25.

Overview of Activities *(cont.)*

5. **Fossils:** Before students can understand the concept of "real" dinosaurs, they must first understand fossils and their formation. Instructions for making, setting up, and rotating through Fossils: Dinosaur File Folder Learning Centers are given on pages 19–26.

6. **Dinosaur Classification:** After comparing the different groups of dinosaurs, students will go one step further and classify the different species into subgroups, using the Dinosaur Classification work sheet on page 27.

7. **Compare and Contrast:** Direct students to read and follow the directions on page 28 to complete a **Dinosaurs Venn Diagram** to compare and contrast characteristics of the two dinosaur groups.

8. **Dinosaur Report:** Develop specific knowledge about a dinosaur of the student's choice with a Dinosaur Report. Students should be divided into groups of two or three to research the dinosaurs. The teacher may elect to have one group report or individual reports from each student. Students should research, write a first draft, edit the draft, make a final copy and then create a cover and title page for their report. The report form on page 29 can be used to write the report.

9. **Are There Living Dinosaurs?** Encourage students to find out more about the rumors of living dinosaurs. Direct the students to create a web of fact versus opinion about the rumors and to write their own opinions about the rumors of "living dinosaurs" after completing the survey "Are There Living Dinosaurs?" on page 30.

EXTENDING THE BOOK

1. **Encourage students to check the library for other books about dinosaurs.** Aliki, the author of *Digging Up Dinosaurs,* has written many books on the subject of dinosaurs and related concepts. Direct the students to write a letter to the author of their favorite books in care of the publisher. Many authors will answer letters.

2. **Culminating Activity:** As a culminating activity let children make some "dinosaur food." This activity will give them experience in reading, understanding, and following directions as well as developing measuring skills. Copy this recipe onto a large chart.

Dinosaur Food

⅛ cup (30 mL) dirt (cocoa)	¼ cup (60 mL) yellow slime (butter)
¼ cup (60 mL) swamp water (milk)	1¼ cup (300 mL) grass (uncooked oatmeal)
¼ cup (60 mL) crushed bones (sugar)	¼ cup (60 mL) squashed bugs (peanut butter)

Mix dirt and swamp water, then add crushed bones and yellow slime. Bring to a boil in medium pan. Boil 1 minute. Remove from heat and stir in grass and squashed bugs. Drop by spoonfuls onto waxed paper until cool and firm.

Dinosaur Egg-citement

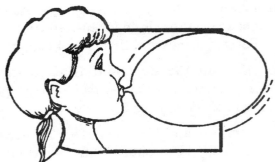

Materials:

    one round, medium-sized balloon
    several sheets of newspaper
    white paper towels
    wheat paste (available at wallpaper stores)
    warm water
    small mixing bowl
    wire mixing whisk
    straight pin
    wrapped candies or treats

Procedure:

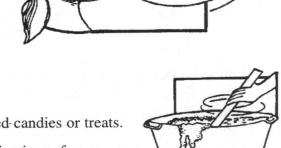

- Fill the uninflated balloon with small wrapped candies or treats.

- Inflate the balloon 8" to 12" (20 cm–30 cm) in circumference.

- Pour one cup (236 mL) of wheat paste into a small mixing bowl.

- Slowly add warm water while stirring with wire whisk. Mix to the consistency of liquid glue.

- Tear the newspaper into 2" x 6" (5 cm x 15 cm) strips. Tear several white paper towels in the same strips.

- Dip a newspaper strip into the paste, keeping it straight. Pull the strip out of the paste through two fingers to remove excess paste.

- Put the strips on the balloon one at a time. Cover the entire balloon with pasted strips.

- Cover the balloon two more times with newspaper strips.

- Cover the newspaper strips on the balloon with white paper towels. The white towels will give the "egg" a white, leathery look.

- Be careful not to get the balloon too wet.

- Let the egg dry completely. This may take two or three days.

- When the egg is completely dry, push the straight pin through the paper and break the balloon.

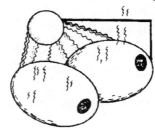

When Will It Hatch?

Make a nest for the egg from straw and sand. Introduce the unit on dinosaurs and tell the students that the egg will hatch when all of the activities are complete. Break the egg open at the end of the unit and share the candy and treats inside.

Dino-Dictionary Skills

Saying words by the sounds each letter or group of letters make is called pronunciation. Entry words in a dictionary show the pronunciation of words in parentheses with symbols over the letters to represent specific sounds.

Directions: Look up the words below in a dictionary and write the pronunciations, with the symbols, on the lines beside the words. Then use the Pronunciation Guide at the bottom of the page to pronounce the words correctly. Read the definitions for each word to see what the word means. Use the Dino-Dictionary page as a reference throughout the unit.

Paleozoic Era _____

Cambrian _____ Ordovician _____

Silurian _____ Devonian _____

Mississippian _____ Pennsylvanian _____

Permian _____

Mesozoic Era _____

Triassic _____ Jurassic _____

Cretaceous _____

Cenozoic Era _____

Tertiary _____ Quaternary _____

Dinosaur Era _____

ornithischian _____ saurischian _____

ornithopoda _____ stegosaur _____

ankylosaur _____ ceratopsia _____

theropod _____ sauropod _____

pelycosaur _____ plesiosaur _____

pterosaur _____ pachycephalosaur _____

bipedal _____ quadruped _____

carnivore _____ omnivore _____

herbivore _____ extinction _____

ectothermic _____ endothermic _____

paleontology _____ paleontologist _____

geologic _____ Pangaea _____

The symbol above each letter stands for a special sound.
The word under each letter tells you how the letter sounds in a word.

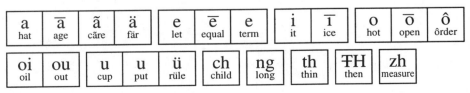

a hat	ā age	ã cãre	ä fär	e let	ē equal	e term	i it	ī ice	o hot	ō open	ô ôrder

oi oil	ou out	u cup	u put	ü rüle	ch child	ng long	th thin	ŦH then	zh measure

ə represents: a in about,
e in taken, i in pencil
o i lemon, u in circus

Digging into Picture Books

Teachers of intermediate grades sometimes undervalue the contribution of easy-to-read picture books in their classrooms. Teachers who use picture books successfully, even though these books are considered too easy for intermediate children, build background knowledge, help children focus on particular ideas or concepts, and help children recognize words that they might encounter later when reading independently on the same subject.

K-W-L Strategy

Brainstorm what is already known and what the students want to learn about fossils and dinosaurs to enable students to learn from each other's knowledge and experiences. List the responses on the KWL Chart and at the end of the unit complete the chart by listing what has been learned.

Dinosaur KWL Chart

What We Know	What We Want to Find Out	What We Have Learned

Illustrations

Teachers may "walk through" *Digging Up Dinosaurs* via the illustrations before actually reading the book to the students. The illustrations are carefully designed to provide children with information they will use to understand the book and to read the related text. They also guide children to use their natural sense of language when talking about pictures to come up with the key words or actual text.

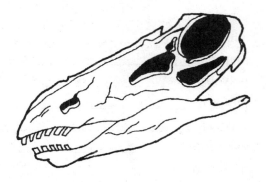

Vocabulary

Teach the vocabulary within the context as the teacher reads the book to the class. This gives the students the benefit of using the illustrations and text content to better understand the words. Use the same strategy to teach ideas and concepts that need to be remembered.

Section by Section

Digging Up Dinosaurs is filled with information about dinosaur fossils and the process used to find and recover them. It is recommended that short sections of the book be read to students, discussed as a group, and then section-specific activities be done as a reinforcement. The following can be used as a discussion tool so that students get the greatest benefit from the book. Attention can be directed toward the information that will be needed to complete the activities following each section.

PAGES 1–8

Early fossil discoveries led scientists to believe that all dinosaurs were enormous, lizard-like creatures. In reality, dinosaurs were all sizes and shapes and all dinosaurs walked with an erect posture unlike that of reptiles. The largest dinosaurs weighed 70 to 80 and measured almost 100 feet long while the smallest was the size of a turkey.

Explain that although the word dinosaur means "terrible lizard," dinosaurs were not lizards. They are grouped in the same class as reptiles because the shape of their skulls and hips resembles that of present-day reptiles and lizards. There are two distinctive dinosaur groups with many different kinds of dinosaurs in each group. Specific groups, bird-hipped or lizard-hipped, had similar characteristics but they also had individual features that made them different. For instance, although Tyrannosaurs and Brachiosaurus belonged to the same saurischian dinosaur (bird-hipped) group, they did not look anything alike.

PAGES 9–24

Dinosaur hunting began in England in the 1820's with the discovery of giant fossilized teeth and a fossil skeleton from the dinosaur, Iguanodon. In 1841 Richard Owen, a comparative anatomist, named the discoveries *Dinosauria,* meaning Terrible Lizard. It wasn't until the 1880's, when dinosaur hunters recovered complete skeletons from the western United States, that scientists recognized that the study of fossilized animal and plant life could trace the evolutionary history of extinct as well as living species. Now specialized teams of experts are used to find and recover remains from sedimentary rock where most fossils are found.

Explain that fossils are the remains or partial remains of a once living organism that have been preserved in rock. Fossils are formed when an organism is buried in mud or sand before the hard parts of its body can decay. Fossils of dinosaur remains tell what dinosaurs looked like, the texture of their skin, how they walked, what kind of food they ate, how large they were, and how they moved. Fossilized eggs tell how they reproduced. Fossils cannot tell what color dinosaurs were or how they behaved but scientists make guesses based on comparisons with living animals with some of the same characteristics.

Section By Section *(cont.)*

PAGES 25–32

There are two major groups of dinosaurs identified by the shape of their hipbones: Ornithischian (or-ni-THISS-kee-an) and Saurischian (saw-RISS-kee-an) dinosaurs. Refer to the Fingertip Fact cards (pages 60–77) for more specific information on dinosaur groups.

Discuss the different dinosaur characteristics as the book is read. Use the Fingertip Fact cards for more information on specific dinosaurs and the meanings of their names. Include the use of the following words and meanings in the discussion.

- bipedal: walked erect on two feet with tail held behind for balance

- quadrupedal: walked on four straight legs (under body)

- carnivore: a meat-eating dinosaur

- herbivore: a plant-eating dinosaur

- omnivore: a dinosaur that ate plants and meat

- Geologic Era: Scientists record time in eras. The science of geology helps record time through the study of fossils.

- Geologic Time Period: A division within an era.

Discuss the **rumors of living dinosaurs** in Africa, the Great Lakes of the United States, and Scotland's Loch Ness. The "monster" of Loch Ness is the most popular "living dinosaur" theory available.

Magnitude Measures

Directions: Solve the problems below to find out the approximate heights, lengths, and weights of different dinosaurs. Then complete the graphs on the pages 14 and 15 to compare the height and weight of several dinosaurs to the height and weight of automobiles and people. Make a poster board graph with a group of other students to show the dinosaurs' weights compared to the weight of an elephant.

Dinosaur Measurements: Height and Length

	Height		*Length*	
Tyrannosaurus	$900 \div 45 =$ _____ feet tall		$3250 \div 65 =$ _____ feet long	
Diplodocus	$6744 \div 281 =$ _____ feet tall		$1260 \div 14 =$ _____ feet long	
Stegosaurus	$1152 \div 72 =$ _____ feet tall		$625 \div 25 =$ _____ feet long	
Brachiosaurus	$2772 \div 63 =$ _____ feet tall		$2975 \div 35 =$ _____ feet long	
Coelophysis	$1284 \div 321 =$ _____ feet tall		$9860 \div 986 =$ _____ feet long	
Triceratops	$8640 \div 720 =$ _____ feet tall		$7025 \div 281 =$ _____ feet long	

Dinosaur Measurements: Weight
2,000 pounds=1 ton   1 elephant= 1 ton

1. Allosaurus, Spinosaurus, and Parasaurolophus each weighed 8,000 pounds. What do these three dinosaurs weigh all together? These dinosaurs weigh _____ pounds all together. How many elephants would it take to weigh the same as Allosaurus, Spinosaurus, or Parasaurolophus? _____ elephants weigh the same.

2. Ankylosaurus, Iguanodon, and Triceratops each weighed 10,000 pounds. What is the weight of Triceratops and Ankylosaurus together? These dinosaurs weigh _____ pounds together. How many elephants would it take to weigh the same as Ankylosaurus, Iguanodon, and Triceratops? _____ elephants weigh the same.

3. Apatosaurus weighed 60,000 pounds. How many elephants would it take to weigh the same as Apatosaurus? _____ elephants weighed the same as Apatosaurus.

4. Brachiosaurus weighed 160,000 pounds. How many elephants would it take to weigh the same as Brachiosaurus? _____ elephants weigh the same as Brachiosaurus.

5. Corythosaurus, Stegosaurus, and Styracosaurus each weighed 6,000 pounds. How much do all three dinosaurs weigh? All three dinosaurs weigh _____ . How many elephants would it take to weigh the same as Corythosaurus, Stegosaurus, or Styracosaurus? _____ elephants weigh the same.

6. Diplodocus weighed 50,000 pounds. How many elephants would it take to weigh the same as Diplodocus? _____ elephants weigh the same as Diplodocus.

7. Pachycephalosaurus weighed 2,000 pounds. How many elephants would it take to weigh the same as Pachycephalosaurus? _____ elephants weigh the same as Pachycephalosaurus.

8. Tyrannosaurus weighed 2,000 pounds. How many elephants would it take to weigh the same as Tyrannosaurus? _____ elephants weigh the same as Tyrannosaurus.

Dinosaur Length Graph

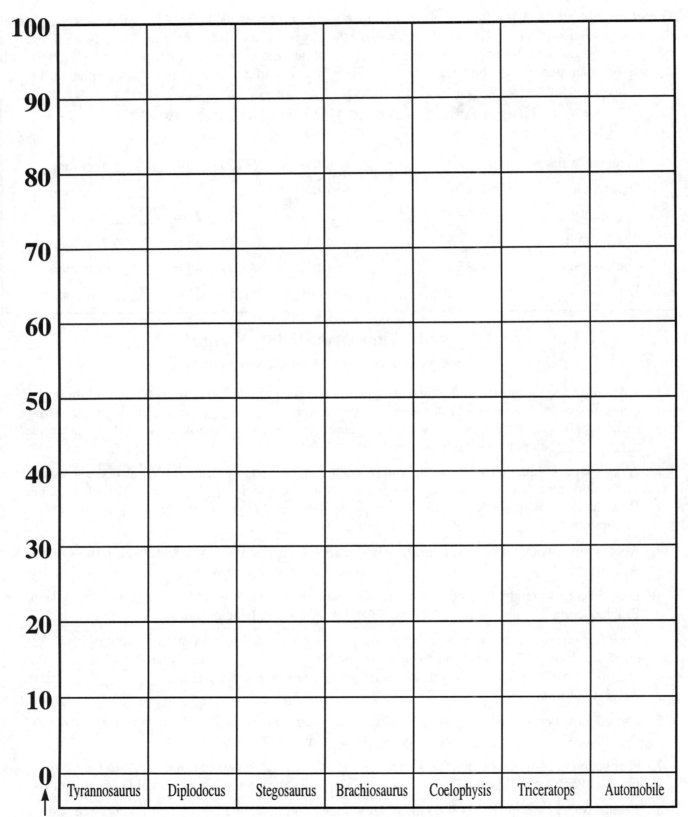

Length in Feet

Dinosaur Height Graph

Height in Feet →

Height in Feet	Tyrannosaurus	Diplodocus	Stegosaurus	Brachiosaurus	Coelophysis	Triceratops	Human
100							
90							
80							
70							
60							
50							
40							
30							
20							
10							

Creature Features

Dinosaurs have many distinctive features. Write a descriptive paragraph about a dinosaur using the Listing Guide below, Creature Feature Words (page 17), and dinosaur pictures from Fingertip Facts (pages 60–67).

Directions:

1. Choose a dinosaur picture.

2. Look carefully at the picture.

3. List three words that describe each part of the dinosaur's body and features. Use the "Creature Feature Words" to help select the best words to use.

4. Write one sentence using one or two words from each list of words.

5. Put the sentences into paragraph order. Begin the paragraph with the main idea sentence, "Dinosaurs have many distinctive features."

6. Give your work a title.

LISTING GUIDE

Directions: List three words that describe each dinosaur body part.

Head	Teeth	Neck
_____	_____	_____
_____	_____	_____
_____	_____	_____

Body	Front Legs	Back Legs
_____	_____	_____
_____	_____	_____
_____	_____	_____

Tail	Other Features
_____	_____
_____	_____
_____	_____

Creature Features *(cont.)*

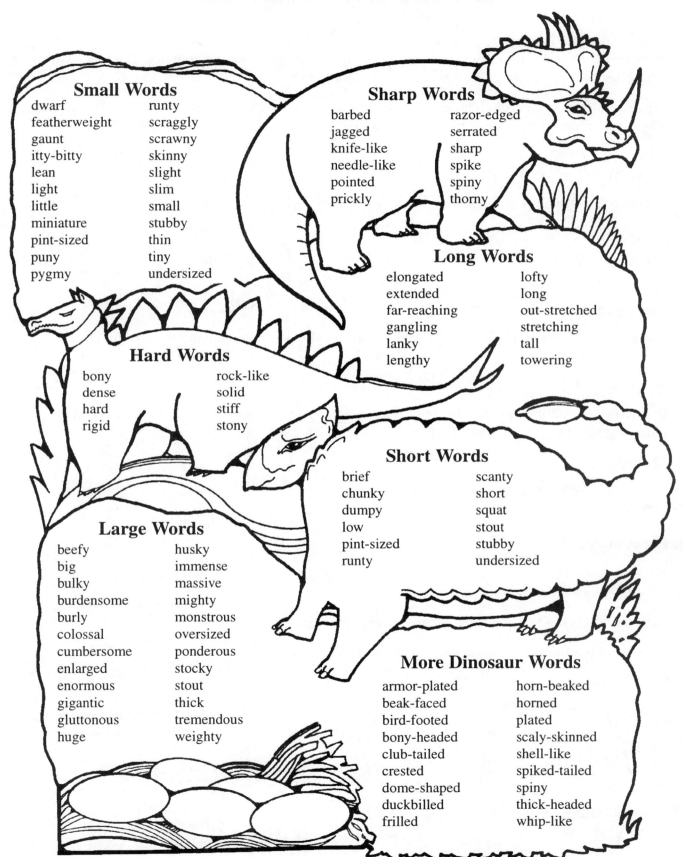

Small Words

dwarf	runty
featherweight	scraggly
gaunt	scrawny
itty-bitty	skinny
lean	slight
light	slim
little	small
miniature	stubby
pint-sized	thin
puny	tiny
pygmy	undersized

Sharp Words

barbed	razor-edged
jagged	serrated
knife-like	sharp
needle-like	spike
pointed	spiny
prickly	thorny

Long Words

elongated	lofty
extended	long
far-reaching	out-stretched
gangling	stretching
lanky	tall
lengthy	towering

Hard Words

bony	rock-like
dense	solid
hard	stiff
rigid	stony

Short Words

brief	scanty
chunky	short
dumpy	squat
low	stout
pint-sized	stubby
runty	undersized

Large Words

beefy	husky
big	immense
bulky	massive
burdensome	mighty
burly	monstrous
colossal	oversized
cumbersome	ponderous
enlarged	stocky
enormous	stout
gigantic	thick
gluttonous	tremendous
huge	weighty

More Dinosaur Words

armor-plated	horn-beaked
beak-faced	horned
bird-footed	plated
bony-headed	scaly-skinned
club-tailed	shell-like
crested	spiked-tailed
dome-shaped	spiny
duckbilled	thick-headed
frilled	whip-like

Dinosaur Hunters

When a dinosaur fossil is discovered many expert people are involved in the tedious process of extracting the fossil bones from stone and reassembling them to make a complete skeleton. One of the most important people is a scientist called a paleontologist.

A paleontologist is a person who studies the fossils of prehistoric animals and plants. These scientists play a major role in unraveling the mystery of dinosaurs and other prehistoric creatures.

Activity I

Experience the tedious process of removing a perfect fossil from stone by "digging for dinosaur bones."

Materials:

- toothpicks
- chocolate chip cookies

Procedure:

Use a toothpick to separate chocolate chips from a cookie without breaking the cookie.

Activity II

Experience the difficult process of finding and correctly reassembling dinosaur bones, using the following activity.

Materials:

- bones from several whole chickens
- clay

Procedure:

Remove all of the meat from chicken bones by boiling the bones until they are clean and clear of any remaining meat. Allow them to dry for several days.

Bury the bones in sand that the students can dig through.

Have them reassemble the bones they find using clay as cement.

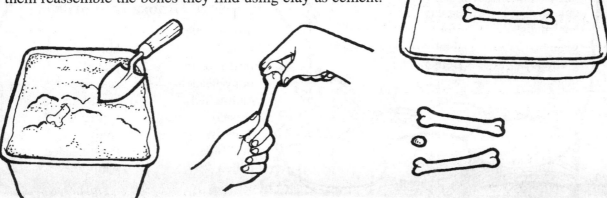

Fossils: File Folder Learning Centers

File folder learning centers are fun and easy to use. Once the folders for the centers are constructed the teacher simply sets them on a table, provides all the necessary materials, starts the rotation, and sets the timer for the allowed time to complete each center. Then the students rotate through the centers and complete the activities through cooperative interaction.

Materials: 9" x 12" (23 cm x 30 cm) colored file folders, rubber cement, crayons, markers, copy of pages 18-24 for all centers, construction paper

Procedures: Duplicate and cut pages 20–26 apart. Open a file folder as you would a book. Glue the "Student Reading" page on the inside left folder. Glue the "Activity Directions" on the inside right folder. Glue on the identifying "File Folder Tabs" (see bottom of this page). Color and decorate with dinosaur pictures and laminate. (Use pictures from Fingertip Facts, pages 60–77).

Mount a completed "Activity Sheet" on construction paper and laminate. Use it to demonstrate center outcomes. Make a copy of the activity sheets for each student set. The centers are then ready for use.

Grouping Students: Divide the class into four or five groups of no more than six students. Explain center rotation and make it clear that students must read and follow the instructions to complete the activities in the center. Assign a group to each center and start the center rotation. Set the timer for 25 minutes. When the bell rings, allow up to 5 minutes for clean-up and then rotate the students clockwise to the next center. Provide books and magazines at centers for students to enjoy if they finish faster than others.

Center Activities: Center activities are self-guiding. More advanced readers should help others with the reading so that all students will be successful

Teacher Help: Teachers should move around the learning centers to answer any questions and make sure all students are actively involved in the learning process.

Listening Center: A reading and listening center can be provided as an extra activity to go along with the concept of centers. Choose any book about fossils or dinosaurs and record it on cassette tape. One child may hold the book and let the other students listen.

File Folder Tabs

Making a Fossil Cast
Fossil Nest
How Fossils Are Formed
Finding Fossils

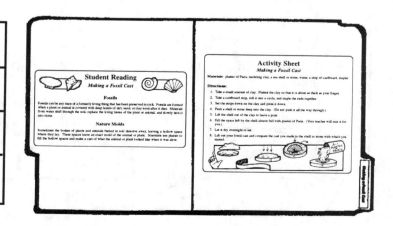

Student Reading
Making a Fossil Cast

Fossils

Fossils can be any trace of a formerly living thing that has been preserved in rock. Fossils are formed when a plant or animal is covered with deep layers of dirt, sand, or clay soon after it dies. Minerals from water shift through the soil, replace the living tissue of the plant or animal, and slowly turn it into stone.

Nature Molds

Sometimes the bodies of plants and animals buried in soil dissolve away, leaving a hollow space where they lay. These spaces leave an exact mold of the animal or plant. Scientists use plaster to fill the hollow spaces and make a cast of what the animal or plant looked like when it was alive.

Activity Sheet
Making a Fossil Cast

Materials: plaster of Paris, modeling clay, a sea shell or stone, water, a strip of cardboard, stapler

Directions:

1. Take a small amount of clay. Flatten the clay so that it is about as thick as your finger.

2. Take a cardboard strip, roll it into a circle, and staple the ends together.

3. Set the strips down on the clay and press it down.

4. Push a shell or stone deep into the clay. (Do not push it all the way through.)

5. Lift the shell out of the clay to leave a print.

6. Fill the space left by the shell almost full with plaster of Paris. (Your teacher will mix it for you.)

7. Let it dry overnight to set.

8. Lift out your fossil cast and compare the cast you made to the shell or stone with which you started.

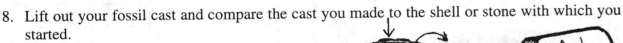
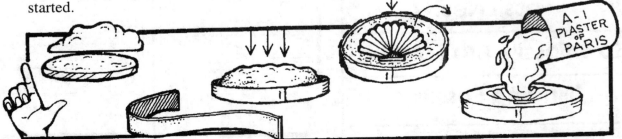

Student Reading
Making a Fossilized Dinosaur Nest

Dinosaur Nest

Scientists believe that most dinosaurs reproduced by laying eggs. Female dinosaurs laid their eggs in nests dug in sand or mud. The eggs were laid in a circle one on top of the other. Each dinosaur laid at least 15 eggs. The size of the eggs were small compared to the huge size of some of the dinosaurs. The largest egg ever found was ten inches (25 cm) long.

Dinosaur Eggs

Just like all other eggs, the eggs of dinosaurs were small and easy to break. Most dinosaur nests have been destroyed by heavy sand or mud over millions of years. But, many nests have been discovered that have complete fossilized eggs in them with the embryos of small dinosaur hatchlings inside.

Activity Directions
Making a Fossilized Dinosaur Nest

Materials: modeling clay, plaster of Paris, paint, 9 or 10 marbles, water, paintbrush, lid from 1/2 gallon ice cream carton

Directions:

1. Take small amount of clay. Flatten the clay so that it is about as thick as your finger.

2. Press the clay into the ice cream lid so that it completely covers the bottom.

3. Press the marbles firmly into the clay, so that they press against the bottom of the lid.

4. Remove the marbles from the clay to leave empty spaces.

5. Pour plaster of Paris into the lid until lit covers the empty spaces. Let the plaster of Paris dry and harden.

6. After it dries, remove the lid and flip it over so that the prints of the marbles show where they were pressed into the clay.

7. Paint your dinosaur nest.

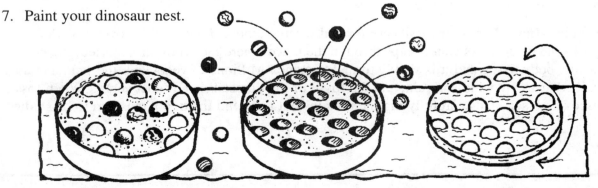

Student Reading

How Fossils Are Formed

Scientists who study things left from life long ago are called "paleontologists" (pay-lee-on-TAHL-o-gists). Many fossils from plants and animals have been found all over the world. The remains of plants and animals that have turned to stone over millions of years tell us what life was like back then. Fossils can tell us much about dinosaurs except their color and habits. Most scientists think that dinosaurs were much the same color as the reptiles today.

Skin Prints: Fossilized skin prints from some dinosaurs show that their skin was rough and covered with scales. Other prints show some dinosaurs were covered with fur or feathers.

Bones: Bone fossils are reassembled to show many things about dinosaurs. Scientists can tell where muscles were connected to the bones and how the dinosaurs moved and whether they walked on two or four feet. The bones show how many fingers or toes were on the dinosaur's hands or feet, and what kinds of claws they had. The height, length, and weight of dinosaurs are also determined by the bones.

Skull: The skull shows the size of the dinosaur's brain. A larger brain usually indicated a smarter animal. The teeth from the skull show the kinds of food the dinosaur ate. The eye sockets were measured to show the size of the eyes and where they were located on the dinosaur's head. Large eyes set at the front of the skull provide better eyesight than small eyes and those located on the side of the head.

Bony Parts: Some dinosaurs had bony structures on parts of their bodies. The frills of the ceratopsian dinosaurs; the plates of the stegosaurs; and the heads, tails, fins, and sails of other dinosaurs were all made from a hard, bone-like material. Scientists believe that these structures could have been used to regulate body temperature, to provide protection, or simply to tell male from female.

Tail: The bones from the tail of a dinosaur show how long it was and how the tail was used. Most dinosaurs held their tails out behind their bodies for balance. Some dinosaurs used their tails as weapons and could swing them from side to side as well as move them up and down.

Footprints: The footprints left by dinosaurs support the belief that they lived in herds. Footprints of many dinosaurs walking together have been discovered all over the world. The footprints show that babies walked along with grown dinosaurs and indicate that dinosaurs took care of their young.

Fossil Formation: Dinosaur fossils are formed when a dinosaur dies and is covered with deep layers of sand or dirt. As water seeps through the place where the dinosaur is buried, minerals replace the body tissue and it is slowly turned to stone. Millions of years later the sand and dirt are washed away by wind and rain, and the fossil of the dinosaur is left uncovered. When fossils are discovered, scientists carefully dig the remains out and send them to a museum to be studied.

Activity Directions
How Fossils Are Formed

Materials: activity sheet, "Word Blocks" labels, crayons, scissors, glue, 9" x 12" (23 cm x 30 cm) construction paper

Directions:

1. Take out Activity Sheet (page 24) and "Word Blocks." Color the pictures.

2. Cut out the pictures and "Word Blocks."

3. Put the pictures in order to show "How Fossils Are Formed." Glue them onto the construction paper in order.

4. Match the sentences to the pictures and glue them under the correct pictures to show "How Fossils Are Formed."

5. Put your name at the top.

Word Blocks

Heavy wind and rain wash away part of the sand and dirt. Then a part of the dinosaur can be seen.	The bones are hidden for millions of years. Water and minerals seep through sand and slowly turn the bones to stone.
A scientist finds the fossil of a dinosaur and carefully digs it out of the stone to take to a museum and study.	The bodies of some of the dinosaurs were covered by sand and dirt after they died.
All the dinosaurs died suddenly 65 million years ago.	Dinosaurs lived on Earth for 160 million years.

Activity Sheet: *How Fossils Are Formed*

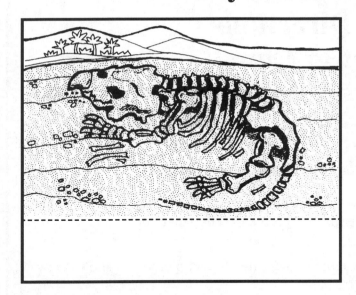

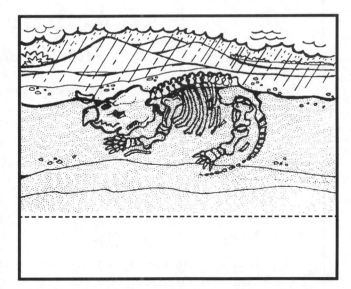

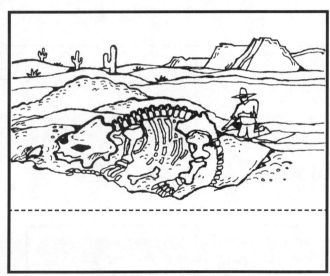

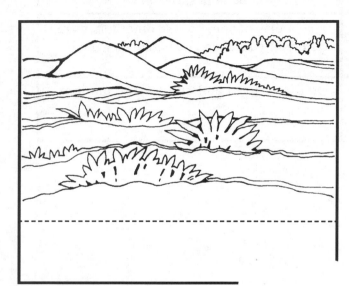

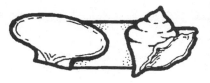

Student Reading
Finding Fossils
Dinosaur Fossils

There were two different kinds of dinosaurs that lived for over 160 million years. Scientists don't know exactly why dinosaurs all died 65 million years ago, but their fossils have been discovered all over the world. These fossils are very important because they tell us about life millions of years before humans lived on Earth.

Where Are Dinosaur Fossils Found?

Dinosaur fossils have been found all over the world. After a dinosaur fossil is discovered, scientists work together on a project called a "dig" in which they slowly take the dinosaur fossils from dirt and rocks. They clean each piece and then send it to a museum so that all the pieces can be put back together and studied. Scientists separate dinosaurs into two groups by the shape of their hipbones. Because the scientific names for dinosaurs are difficult to remember, they are usually referred to as "bird-hipped" or "lizard-hipped" dinosaurs.

Ornithischian Dinosaurs (or-ni-THISS-kee-an)

Ornithischian dinosaurs had hipbones shaped like the hips of present-day birds. All of these dinosaurs were plant eaters, all had hoofed-toes, and all except one had beak-like mouths. Some of this group walked on two legs and others walked on four legs. The five subgroups identified as ornithischian dinosaurs are stegosaurs (steg-uh-sawrs), ankylosaurs (ang-kee-loh-sawrs), ceratopsias (sair-uh-top-see-uhs), ornithopodas (or-nith-aw-pod-uhs), and pachycephalosaurs (pak-ee-sef-uh-lo-sawrs).

Saurischian Dinosaurs (saw-RISS-kee-an)

Saurischian dinosaurs had hipbones shaped like the hips of present-day lizards. All of these dinosaurs had clawed feet. The smallest and largest dinosaurs were members of this group. These dinosaurs included plant eaters and meat eaters and dinosaurs that walked on two or four legs. The two subgroups identified as saurischian dinosaurs are theropodas (thair-aw-pod-ahs) and sauropodas (sawr-aw-pod-ahs).

Activity Directions
Finding Fossils

Reproduce maps for students. Provide red, blue, and green crayons.

Activity Sheet: *Finding Fossils*

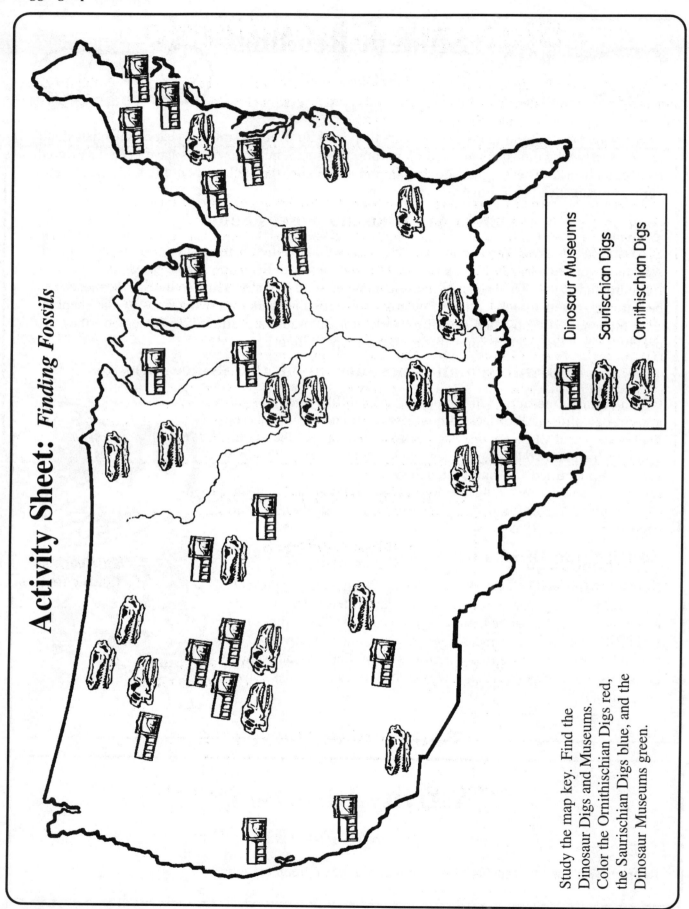

Study the map key. Find the Dinosaur Digs and Museums. Color the Ornithischian Digs red, the Saurischian Digs blue, and the Dinosaur Museums green.

Dinosaur Museums

Saurischian Digs

Ornithischian Digs

26

Dinosaur Classification

Directions: Read the dinosaur descriptions with the boldfaced clues to help you classify the different dinosaur species into their correct subgroups. Use the diagram below to set up your paper and write the names of the dinosaurs under their subgroup heading.

Dinosaur Descriptions

Ankylosaurus had sharp spikes protruding from the bony, shell-like **armor** that protected its body.

Tyrannosaurs had huge legs and large **beast-like feet** with razor sharp claws on each toe.

Corythosaurus had a helmet shaped crest on its head. It walked erect on two strong hind legs and small **bird-like feet.**

Spinosaurus had a six-foot long (1.8 m) spiny sail running along its back. Its feet were large and beast-like.

Iguanodon had small **bird-like feet** and short arms that held four fingers and a sharp, spiked thumb.

Pachycephalosaurus had a **thick,** bony dome-shaped plate covering its head with knobs and sharp spikes on its nose.

Parasaurolophus had a pointed, six-foot-long (1.8 m) crest on its head. It had small, strong legs with **bird-like feet.**

Stegosaurus had two rows of **bony, leaf-shaped plates** running from behind its neck to the middle of its tail.

Styracosaurus had a large head with a two-foot-long (60 cm) **sharp horn on its nose.** Its frill held six sharp spikes.

Triceratops had **two sharp horns** over its eyebrows and **one shorter horn** on its nose.

Allosaurus had powerful jaws with long sharp teeth. Each **beast-like foot** had three toes with sharp claws.

Apatosaurus had huge **lizard-like feet** and strong heavy legs that carried its thirty-ton weight.

Brachiosaurus weighed eighty tons. Its heavy legs and **lizard-like feet** supported the tremendous weight of its body.

Coelophysis was one of the smallest dinosaurs. Its neck and tail were long and thin and its **beast-like feet** were small.

Diplodocus was the longest dinosaur. Its huge, heavy legs and **lizard-like feet** carried twenty-five tons of weight.

Ornithischian Dinosaurs

Pachycephalosaur
(thick-headed reptile)

_____

Ornithopoda
(bird-footed reptiles)

_____

_____

_____

Ceratopsia
(horn-faced reptiles)

_____

_____

Stegosaur
(plated reptile)

_____

Ankylosaur
(armor-covered reptile)

_____

Saurischian Dinosaurs

Sauropoda
(lizard-footed reptile)

_____

_____

_____

Theropoda
(beast-like reptiles)

_____

_____

_____

Dinosaurs Venn Diagram

Directions: Draw a Venn diagram on another piece of paper using the model on this page as a guide. Read the dinosaur facts below and use the information to complete a dinosaur Venn diagram by writing each statement below in the correct section of the intersecting circles.

- had hipbones shaped like those of a bird
- had hipbones shaped like those of a lizard
- included plant and meat eaters
- were both large and small
- lived all over the world
- were all plant eaters

- lived during Mesozoic Era
- has five subgroups
- had clawed feet
- has two subgroups
- had hoofed toes
- had beak-like mouths

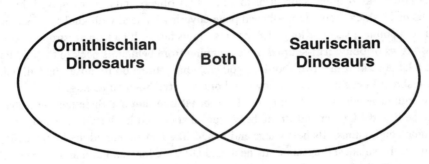

Challenge: Pelycosaurs, Plesiosaurs, and Pterosaurs all lived in the same time periods as dinosaurs. Make a Venn diagram to compare their characteristics with those of dinosaurs.

Dinosaur Facts

Dinosaur is the name given to two distinct groups of animals that are now extinct. They were given the Greek name *deinos sauros*, meaning "terrible lizard" because early fossil discoveries led scientists to believe that they were all giant-sized and lizard-like. Fossil remains from both groups have been found all over the world. Both dinosaur groups lived during the Mesozoic Era. They had common characteristics, such as scaly skin and reptile-like skulls and walked in an erect posture like present-day mammals. They did not crawl along the ground, with legs spread, as reptiles.

Saurischian Dinosaurs

Saurischian dinosaurs had hipbones shaped like the hipbones of present-day lizards. All of these dinosaurs had clawed feet. Saurischian dinosaurs included herbivores and carnivores. Some were bipedal with short arms and others were quadrupedal. Fossils of the smallest and largest dinosaurs found come from this group. There are two subgroups of saurischian dinosaurs—theropoda and sauropoda.

Ornithischian Dinosaurs

Ornithischian dinosaurs had hipbones shaped like the hipbones of present-day birds. All of these dinosaurs were herbivores. They all had hoofed toes and all, except one, had beaked mouths. Some of this group were bipedal and others were quadrupedal. There are five subgroups of ornithischian dinosaurs—ornithopoda, ceratopsia, stegosaur, ankylosaur, and pachycephalosaur.

Dinosaur Report

Name of Dinosaur: _____

Group Classification: _____
(ornithischian - bird-hipped) (saurischian - lizard-hipped)

Subgroup Classification: _____
(ornithopoda, ceratopsia, stegosaur, ankylosaur, theropoda, sauropoda, pachycephalosaur, plesiosaur, pterosaur, pelycosaur)

Bipedal or Quadrupedal: _____

Carnivore, Herbivore, or Omnivore: _____

Height: _____

Weight: _____

Length: _____

Illustration

Geological Era: _____

Geological Time Period: _____

Important facts and description of dinosaur:

_____

_____

_____

_____

_____

_____

_____

_____

_____

_____

_____

_____

_____

Report Completed by: _____

Are There Living Dinosaurs?

Directions: Read the following paragraphs. Compare the mystery of Loch Ness with the facts about marine reptiles by answering yes or no to the "Fact or Opinion Survey." Draw your own conclusions about "living dinosaurs" and write a short paragraph explaining the reasons why you do or do not believe that they really exist.

Mystery of Loch Ness

Loch Ness is a large lake in Northern Scotland. It is 24 miles (38.4 km) long, and 1 mile (1.6 km) wide, and its deepest point is 750 feet (230 m). It cuts across Scotland and joins the Atlantic Ocean and the North Sea. The lake is rumored to have a sea monster living within its depths. The creature, reported to be at least 30 feet (9 m) long, has been seen many times in Loch Ness. Some of the first sightings were reported as early as the 500s and many people reported seeing the monster during the 1930s. People who have claimed to see the creature say that it has a long neck and tail and a wide, round body. Recently, very few sightings have occurred but the rumor of "living dinosaurs" has persisted and has been the focus of much scientific study. Conclusions reached by the scientific community have not been able to prove the rumors one way or the other leaving the question, "Are there really living dinosaurs in Loch Ness?" open to further debate.

Facts About Marine Reptiles

Marine reptiles lived in the same time period as the dinosaur. They lived in the open oceans and moved through the water with flippers similar to those found on present-day turtles. Some scientists believe that they were able to move about on land as walruses do today. There were two kinds of marine reptiles: plesiosaurs and pliosauroids. Plesiosaurs had very long necks, long tails, and slender, round bodies. Pliosauroids had large heads, short necks, long tails, and huge whale-like bodies. They were both carnivores and ate mainly fish.

FACT VS. OPINION SURVEY

1. Does the Loch Ness Monster fit the description of a marine reptile?_____

2. Does the Loch Ness Monster live in the same environment as marine reptiles? _____

3. Is there an adequate food supply in the lake to support an animal of such vast size? _____

4. Is the lake deep enough to hide a creature of such size? _____

5. If there is one creature in the lake, could it be possible that there might be more?_____

6. Is it possible that the creature could swim out into the open sea and not be seen for long periods of time and then appear again? _____

7. Is it possible for such a creature to exist without scientists finding solid evidence to prove it?

   _____

8. Based on the information above, do you believe that there is a dinosaur living in Loch Ness?

   _____

The Magic School Bus® in the Time of the Dinosaurs

by Joanna Cole

Summary

The Magic School Bus® in ihe Time of the Dinosaurs is a fictional account of Ms. Frizzle's class trip back in time to learn more about dinosaurs. The book is filled with accurate information for reading and teaching about dinosaurs and related concepts. It is one book in The Magic School Bus® series that describes a "wacky" teacher who uses extraordinary methods to teach her students.

As the school bus travels back in time the children visit the Mesozoic Era and the dinosaurs that lived during the Mesozoic's three time periods. The simple, child written inserts on each page are easy to understand and the colorful illustrations will peak the curiosity and interest of every student.

The outline below is a suggested plan for using the various activities that are presented in this unit. You should adapt these ideas to fit your own classroom situation.

Sample Plan

Day I

- Introduce the Bulletin Board Map (page 32).
- Set up the Dinosaur Puzzle Center (page 32).
- Brainstorm and write about Time Machines; Build a Time Machine for homework. (page 32)
- Explore the World Wide Web using Dinosaur Web Sites (page 53).
- Read *The Magic School Bus® in the Time of the Dinosaurs.*

Day II

- Begin Section by Section reading (11 pages).
- Identify Vertebrate and Invertebrate Animals (page 32).
- Find and reassemble chicken bones using clay as cement (page 32).
- Dig for fossils using cookies and toothpicks (page 33).
- Identify Dinosaur Names (page 33).

Day III

- Read second section of the book (10 pages).
- Make Pangaea Pastry (page 33).
- Do Earth Vegetation Map on (page 33).
- Illustrate vertebrate egg embryos (page 33).

Day IV

- Read the third section of the book (15 pages).
- Complete Dinosaur Defenses (page 33) and Feathered Reptiles (page 33).
- Complete Are There Living Dinosaurs?
- Make an Time Line (page 33) Dinosaurs?"

Day V

- Read the last section of the book.
- Make a Dinosaur Big Book (page 33).
- Plan a Ms. Frizzle or Visitor's Day as a culminating activity. Make cover and title page.
- Make Dinosaur Food (page 7).

Overview of Activities

SETTING THE STAGE

1. **Bulletin Board Map:** Create a bulletin board using the illustrations on page 41 to show how the Earth looked when it was one giant continent (Pangaea), and the way it looked during the Jurassic and Cretaceous time periods. As the book is read, refer to the bulletin board to explain the concept of Pangaea and the changing world of the dinosaurs. Another bulletin board is found at the end of the overview.

2. **Dinosaur Puzzle Center:** Set up a puzzle center that can be used during the unit. Using any picture of a dinosaur, mount it onto heavy paper. Cut it out and then cut it into several pieces to create puzzles.

3. **Time Machine:** Brainstorm what it would be like to travel back in time to live when dinosaurs were the dominant life form. Discuss what a time machine might look like. Direct the students to write a story using the ideas gathered during the brainstorming. Have them draw the time machine they would use and illustrate their story. Teachers may elect to have the students construct a time machine as a homework assignment to display along with their story on Visitors Day.

4. **Explore the World Wide Web** using the Dinosaur Web Sites listed on page 53. Many of the sites have pictures and sounds that can be downloaded for use in classrooms. Students will enjoy finding new sites on the WWW by following the directions given on page 53.

ENJOYING THE BOOK

1. **Section by Section:** *The Magic School Bus® in the Time of the Dinosaurs* contains the book text, dialog of the characters and inserts on each page that give factual information about dinosaurs and related subjects. It is recommended that the book be read through once and then read one or two segments at a time, discussed as a group, and activities that are section specific be sued with each segment. The section by section guide on pages 35–36 is one usable method.

2. **Vertebrate and Invertebrate Animals:** Use the worksheets on pages 38 and 39 to categorize animals by group, subgroup, name, and picture after modeling the procedure with a group.

3. **Paleontologist:** Remove all of the meat from chicken bones. Boil the bones until they are clean and clear of any remaining meat. Allow them to dry for several days. Bury the bones in sand that the students can dig through and have them reassemble the bones they, find using clay as cement.

Overview of Activities *(cont.)*

4. **Dinosaur Dig:** Allow students to experience the tedious process of removing a fossil by "digging for dinosaur bones". Have them use a toothpick to separate chocolate chips from a cookie without breaking the cookie.

5. **Dinosaur Names:** Scientists use characteristics and particular body features to identify and name dinosaurs. Page 40 can be used to identify the generic names of dinosaurs in the same way.

6. **Pangaea Pastry:** To demonstrate the break-up of the super continent Pangaea and the formation of the continents as we know them today, students can make a pastry shaped like Pangaea and then divide it to show the separation of the continents. (See page 41)

7. **Climate and Vegetation:** Complete the map on page 42 to show the four major climate and vegetation areas on Earth. Encourage the students to compare climates to see which one would most likely be suitable for dinosaurs.

8. **Eggs and Embryos:** Assign groups of students to illustrate embryos inside the eggs of different vertebrate animal species and then compare the drawings to determine the relationships among vertebrate animals.

9. **Predator vs. Prey:** Most animals are armed with special characteristics that help them defend themselves when a predator attacks. Use page 45 to match dinosaurs with the defenses they used against enemies.

10. **Feathered Reptiles:** The first fossil to be identified as a real bird was discovered in Bavaria, Germany. Page 46 gives detailed information about the characteristics that connect Archaeopteryx and early carnivorous dinosaurs. Have the children draw their own interpretation of the bird based on the descriptions of the bird.

11. **Are There Living Dinosaurs?:** Allow students to draw conclusions and write their own opinion about the rumors of "living dinosaurs" after completing the survey "Are There Living Dinosaurs" on page 30.

12. **Time Line:** Make a time line of the animals that lived in the eras and time periods of Earth (pages 48–50). Direct the students to answer the Time Line Questions after completing the time line.

EXTENDING THE BOOK

1. **Ms. Frizzle Day:** Have a "Wacky Mr./Ms. Frizzle Day" when teacher and students wear silly clothes that might be worn by the character, Ms. Frizzle, in The Magic School Bus® stories.

2. **Visitor's Day:** Plan a Dinosaur Visitors Day to show all the activities and projects completed during the unit. Have students make dinosaur invitations to invite parents and community members to attend.

3. **Dinosaur Big Book:** Making Big Books is an excellent way for students to practice their language skills and knowledge of concepts. Use the Big Book idea and directions on page 51 to make a class Big Book.

4. **Resource Personnel:** Contact a local college, university, or museum to see if paleontologists or other experts in the field are on staff. Ask them to visit your classroom and talk to your students.

5. **Field Trips:** Visit a museum with fossils of dinosaurs on display or a dinosaur excavation site for an exciting field trip.

Overview of Activities *(cont.)*

EXTENDING THE ACTIVITIES *(cont.)*

6. **Dinosaur Bulletin Board:** This bulletin board is to introduce, discriminate, compare, and contrast the dinosaurs and other prehistoric animals and to explore the plant life that existed during the Mesozoic Era.

Materials: colored bulletin board paper, stapler, scissors, two small envelopes, 3" x 5" (8 cm x 13 cm), index cards, push pins, Fingertip Facts cards (pages 60–77), and creative writing topics (page 54). Optional: cut letters

Procedure:

1. Copy, cut out and laminate all of the dinosaur and plant pictures from Fingertip Facts onto index cards. Note: The pictures may be colored with markers before laminating.

2. Line the bulletin board with colored paper, staple, and cut to fit.

3. Write the headings or staple the cut letters on the board as in the example above.

4. Staple the dinosaur and plant pictures in place under the correct heading.

5. Copy and glue the Fingertip Facts and Creative Writing Topics on the index cards and laminate.

6. Write "Fingertip Facts" on one envelope and "Creative Writing Topics" on the other. Staple the envelopes in place on the board. Put the appropriate index cards in the envelopes.

7. Line the bottom of the board with the push pins.

Student Directions:

1. Have student pairs practice together. One student reads the Fingertip Facts and the other matches the card to the correct dinosaur or plant. When the answer is agreed upon by both students, they use a push pin to attach the card to the dinosaur or plant that it represents.

2. Students may use the writing topics anytime, or they can be assigned by the teacher as a creative writing assignment.

Section by Section

The Magic School Bus® in the Time of the Dinosaurs is full of factual information for teaching about dinosaurs and associated concepts. It is recommended that section-specific activities be done after reading short segments of the book to reinforce the concepts. The Section by Section guide below can be used as a discussion tool as the book is read. Use and adapt these ideas to fit your program.

Prehistoric: Dinosaurs lived during "prehistoric" time. There were no people to write down or record what happened when dinosaurs ruled the Earth. They lived in an era of time before there were people to record history. We learn about prehistoric dinosaurs through the study of fossils.

Special Reptiles: Dinosaurs were a special group of prehistoric reptiles that had backbones, scaly skin, and reproduced by laying eggs. Discuss the process used by scientists to divide animals into groups by the common characteristics they possess. Vertebrate (animals with backbones) and invertebrate (animals without backbones) include over one million different species. Dinosaurs were all vertebrate animals.

Warm or Cold Blooded: Discuss the differences in warm-blooded (endothermic) and cold-blooded (ectothermic) animals. Explain that all present day reptiles are cold-blooded, have backbones, scaly skin, and walk with their legs sprawled out, making it difficult to move very fast. Reptiles lay eggs but do not care for their young after they are born. Dinosaurs walked with their legs straight under their body (as mammals do). They lived and hunted in herds and cared for and protected their young. Because these characteristics are found only in warm-blooded animals, most scientists believe that dinosaurs were warm-blooded and could control the temperature of their bodies without help from the sun.

Fossils: Scientists called **paleontologists** find out about dinosaurs from fossils. Dinosaur fossils have been found all over the world. After a dinosaur fossil is discovered, scientists work together on a project called a "dig" in which they slowly take the dinosaur fossils from dirt and rocks. They clean each piece and then send it to a museum so that all the pieces can be carefully put back together and studied.

Dinosaur Names: Paleontologists who discover a new dinosaur fossil give it a scientific name with two parts, a generic name and a specific name. The generic name is like a person's last name and is written first and always capitalized. The specific name is like a person's first name. It is written second and not capitalized *(Tyrannosaurs rex)*. Both names are underlined or italicized. Because some dinosaurs are closely related they have the same generic or last name.

Section by Section *(cont.)*

Scientists use several ways to name dinosaurs. The generic names usually identify a particular body feature or a characteristic of the dinosaur. The specific name might identify the person who found the fossil or where it was found. Diplodocus carnegie was named for the "Y shaped" vertebrae in its tail and for Andrew Carnegie, who paid for the expedition that discovered the dinosaur.

Super Continent: Pangaea (pan-Jee-uh) is the name of the land mass or continent that existed one hundred forty-five million years ago. During the late Jurassic Period, when dinosaurs were the dominant life form, Pangaea began to break up and drift apart. As the land was separated by the sea, into the two large continents of Laurasia (lor-AY-shah) and Gondwanaland (gond-WAH-nuh-land), the dinosaurs were scattered all over the Earth. Over millions of years the land drifted further apart little by little until the Earth looked as it does today. The dinosaurs had all died by the time the continents were positioned as they are now.

Climate Regions: The amount and kind of vegetation in a particular area determines what animals can survive there. The prehistoric climate of the dinosaur world was probably related most to hot, tropical forest and swamp lands with plenty of lush vegetation. Extinction of the dinosaurs began about the same time climates changed. The plant-eating dinosaurs had less to eat and began to die out. As in any food chain, the meat-eating dinosaurs also began to die from lack of food.

Five basic climate and vegetation zones exist on Earth today.

Hot and Humid: Rain Forest and savanna
Mild and Humid: Mixed forest and grassland
Cold and Humid: Needle-Leaf and mixed forest
Dry: Desert
Polar and Alpine: Tundra

Egg Embryos: Explain that vertebrate embryos all pass through similar stages as they develop inside eggs. Each vertebrate animal has a notochord at their back with a hollow nerve cord above. This notochord develops into vertebrate, connective tissue, muscle, and, finally, the larger body glands.

Predators and Prey: All animals are dependent life forms. Herbivores, plant eaters, rely on vegetation for food. Carnivores, meat eaters, eat the herbivores. Plant-eating and meat-eating dinosaurs were armed with special characteristics to help them survive in the prehistoric world.

Ankylosaurs had hard, **shell-like plates** covering their body. The plates were made of material similar to the shells of turtles and were very hard to penetrate.

Ceratopian dinosaurs with their long, sharp horns and bony shields posed a formidable threat for any predator.

Claws were common on the carnivorous **theropod** dinosaurs. The lethal curved claw on the feet of the raptor and troodon dinosaurs were used to slash deadly wounds into prey animals so that they would quickly bleed to death. The sharp claws on the hands were used to catch and hold prey while they tore it apart with their teeth.

Section by Section *(cont.)*

A thick, bone-like **helmet** covered the head of the **pachycephalosaurs.** The helmet held sharp spikes and was lowered to meet the threat of predators.

The **stegasaurs** could swing their **sharp, spiked tails** toward enemies to protect themselves. The hard, **bony plates** running from head to tail also helped to protect them from harm.

The **enormous size** of the **sauropod** dinosaurs along with their long, **whip-like tails** was enough to protect them against carnivores.

Dinosaurs to Birds: Some scientists believe that birds are the living relatives of dinosaurs. The fossil remains of the first birds, Archaeopteryx, is a mixture of bird-like and dinosaur characteristics. The backbone was extended to form a long, lizard-like tail and feathers grew over the entire body. Skeletal features resemble modern birds but, unlike present day birds, Archaeopteryx had teeth.

Discuss the **rumors of living dinosaurs** in Africa, the Great Lakes of the United States, and Scotland's Loch Ness. The "monster" of Loch Ness is the most popular "living dinosaur" theory available.

Many animals lived during the same time periods as the dinosaurs. Some are mistakenly called dinosaurs when in fact they were pterosaurs (TAIR-uh-SAWRS), flying reptiles; and plesiosaurs (PLEE-zee-oh-SAWRS), marine reptiles. The first mammals also lived during the same time. Some species died along with the dinosaurs while others survived and flourished.

Marine reptiles called **plesiosaurs** lived in the seas of the ancient world. They were about the size of modern whales but had short bodies, long tails and necks, and flippers. Some scientists believe that these animals could leave the water and move around on land the way sea turtles do today.

Pterosaurs were reptiles with wings that could glide on air currents and use their clawed fingers to climb trees. Some of these bird-like reptiles were smaller than sparrows and others had six feet wing spans. All pterosaurs had reptile heads, hollow bones, and no tail. Some had teeth and a tall crest on their heads and others had no teeth at all.

Discuss eras and time periods as they are recorded by geologists.

> **Mesozoic Era (mez-uh-ZO-ik):** The Mesozoic Era is known as the "Age of the Dinosaurs." It is divided into three separate time periods: the Triassic, the Jurassic, and the Cretaceous.

> **Triassic (try-ASS-ik):** The Triassic was the first time period in the Mesozoic Era. Dinosaurs developed near the end of the Triassic Period that began 225 million years ago.

> **Jurassic (jer-ASS-ik):** The Jurassic time period was the middle time period of the Mesozoic Era. It began 190 million years ago. Large numbers of dinosaurs inhabited the Earth during that time.

> **Cretaceous (kreh-TAY-shus):** The last time period in the Mesozoic Era beginning 135 million years ago. The dinosaurs had all disappeared from Earth by the end of the Cretaceous period that ended 65 million years ago.

Vertebrate and Invertebrate Animals

All animals are classified into two major groups: vertebrate and invertebrate. Vertebrate animals include all animals that have a backbone or spine. Invertebrate animals include all animals without a backbone or spine. Classify the animals below into vertebrate/invertebrate groups, then into a subgroup, then by the name of the animal, and finally by the picture of the animal. (Cut out the picture and glue it to the chart.) Use the words from the word box to help identify the animals.

Word Box

Animal Subgroups

- Mammal
- Bird
- Reptile
- Dinosauria
- Fish
- Amphibian
- Insect
- Snail
- Spider
- Crustacean
- Worm
- Centipede/Millipede

Animal Names

- dragonfly
- earthworm
- thousand leg
- brown spider
- protoceratops
- duck
- conch
- snake
- raccoon
- catfish
- lobster
- frog

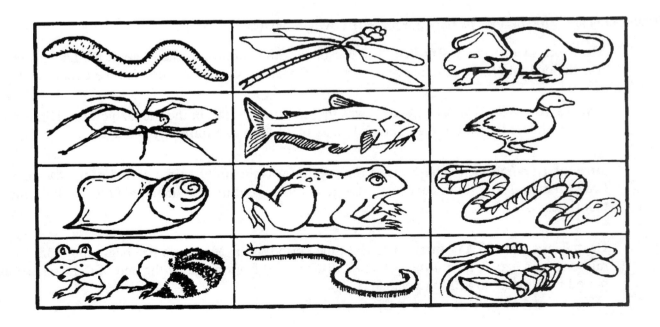

Vertebrate and Invertebrate Animals Chart

Major Group	Subgroup	Name	Picture

Dinosaur Names

Dinosaurs are given generic names based on a particular body feature or characteristic. Generic names have at least two parts with a Latin or Greek meaning. For instance the Greek meaning for dino (deinos) is terrible + saur (sauros) meaning lizard equals the name dinosaur or "terrible lizard." Any combination of the names might be used to name a dinosaur.

I. Use the Generic Name Key below to find out what some of the most popular dinosaur names mean.

II. Pretend you have just discovered the fossil of a new, never discovered dinosaur. First give the dinosaur a generic name using the meanings below; give the dinosaur a specific name by adding your name; last draw a picture of the dinosaur. (Example: Deinoskeratosraptor daniel = terrible horned robber discovered by Daniel)

Tyrannosaurs	*tyrannos + sauros*	_____
Deinonychus	*deinos + onychos*	_____
Allosaurus	*allos + sauros*	_____
Brachiosaurus	*bracchium + sauros*	_____
Troodon	*troo + odontos*	_____
Corythosaurus	*korythos + sauros*	_____
Diplodocus	*diplos + dokos*	_____
Iguanodon	*odontos + iguana*	_____
Maiasaura	*maia + sauros*	_____
Parasaurolophus	*para + lophos + sauros*	_____
Ankylosaurus	*ankyloein + sauros*	_____
Stegosaurus	*stegos + sauros*	_____
Coelophysis	*koilos + physis*	_____
Styracosaurus	*styrax + sauros*	_____
Apatosaurus	*apatelos + sauros*	_____
Triceratops	*tri + keratos+ ops + sauros*	_____
Velociraptor	*velocis + raptor*	_____

Generic Name Key

allos = different	*onychos* = claw
ankyloein = stiffened	*ops* = face
apatelos = deceptive	*pachys* = thick
bracchium = arm	*para* = similar
deinos = terrible	*physis* = form
diplos = double	*raptor* = robber
dokos = beam	*sauros* = lizard
Iguana = like an Iguana	*stegos* = covered or plated
keratos = horned	*stryax* = spiked
koilos = hollow	*tri* = three
korythos = helmet	*troo* = wounding
lophos = crested	*tyrannos* = tyrant
maia = good mother	*velocis* = swift
odontos = teeth	

Pangaea

Two hundred and forty-five million years ago the land on the earth was all joined together in one big mass or continent. This continent was called Pangaea (pan-JEE-uh). Scientists have found no fossils to show that there were any forms of animals life on Earth during this time. Scientist believe that Pangaea began to break up and drift apart during the late Triassic Time Period just as dinosaurs were increasing in numbers. As the land was separated by the sea into the two large continents of Laurasia (lor-AY-shah) and Gondwanaland (gond-WAH-nuh-land), the dinosaurs were scattered over both continents. Many kinds of dinosaurs developed and they ruled the entire Earth. Over millions of years the land drifted further apart, little by little, until the Earth looked as it does now. The dinosaurs had all died by the time the continents were positioned as we know them today.

Figure 1

The way the Earth probably looked during the early part of the Triassic Period when it was one large land mass.

Figure 2

The way the Earth probably looked at the end of the Triassic Period when the continent of Pangaea had drifted into two large land masses called Laurasia and Gondwanaland.

Figure 3

By the end of the Mesozoic Era, when all the dinosaurs disappeared, the Earth probably looked much as it does today.

Pangaea Pastry

To demonstrate the break-up of Pangaea into the continents, use the recipe to make pastry in the shape of the super continent, Pangaea.

Materials: 1 roll refrigerated sugar cookie dough, pastry roller, non-stick vegetable spray, pizza pan, toaster oven (optional: green and blue sprinkles)

Directions: Roll out the premixed cookie dough into the shape of a circle with the pastry roller. Spray the bottom of the pizza pan with non-stick vegetable spray. Spread the cookie dough in the pan so that it touches the sides of the pan and makes a circle. Use the pictures above to divide Pangaea Pastry until it looks like Figure 1. Bake in toaster oven for the recommended time on cookie package. Decorate the land with green sprinkles and the water with blue sprinkles. Note: Divide cookies into smaller pans for cooking if necessary.

Climate and Vegetation Regions

Hot/Humid ☐ Mild/Humid ☐ Cold/Humid ☐ Dry ☐ Polar/Alpine ☐

Dinosaur fossils have been found on every continent of the world. Most dinosaurs were very large and needed a lot of food. Plant-eating dinosaurs probably moved from place to place to find vegetation. The meat-eating dinosaurs moved around, too, following their food supply.

The map shows where the climate and vegetation would be suitable for dinosaurs to live today. Use an atlas to help discover where dinosaurs might live if they were still alive.

Use colored pencils to complete the map by coloring the climate as indicated below.

1. Hot/Humid—Green   2. Mild/Humid—Red   3. Cold/Humid—Orange   4. Dry—Brown   5. Polar/Alpine—Blue

Discovering Kelp

Kelp or brown algae is the largest form of seaweed. Some species can reach a length of 213 feet (65 m). Kelp, as well as other seaweeds, do not have stems, roots, leaves, or vascular systems to transport nutrients. They manufacture their food by photosynthesis and absorb nutrients directly from the water. Fossils of kelp and other algae show that it grew abundantly in the warm, shallow seas of the Mesozoic Era and was probably a major food source for plant eating dinosaurs.

Kelp is rich in vitamins and minerals and a staple food in some diets especially in Japan. Kelp was once the main source for iodine and sodium but is now harvested for the manufacture of **alginic** acid. Unscramble the words below to discover the many uses of kelp.

1. cicomest _____ a substance designed to improve the appearance of skin, hair, etc.

2. shpoil _____ a substance used to make an object shiny and bright

3. anitp _____ a substance applied with a brush or roller as a protective finish or to decorate wood and other surfaces

4. lifm _____ a sheet or roll of flexible cellulose used for taking photographs

5. egl _____ a jellylike substance

6. nolilume _____ a smooth, washable floor covering

7. rrbbeu _____ an elastic substance that is used to make automobile tires, electrical insulation, and elastic bands

8. idneio _____ a substance used as an antiseptic, in the manufacture of dyes, in photography and combined with sodium to make common table salt

9. daso _____ a soft, white compound used with other materials to make table salt, antacids, and preservatives, etc.

10. galni _____ a substance used as a collide to keep ice cream from crystallizing

Word Box

algin	gel	linoleum	polish	soda
film	iodine	cosmetic	rubber	paint

Eggs and Embryos

Animals are divided into two major groups; vertebrate, animals with backbones and invertebrate, animals without backbones. Dinosaurs were vertebrate animals. All vertebrate animals go through similar stages of development as embryos. The notochord develops into vertebrate, connective tissue, muscle, and then into larger body glands. Humans are mammals, and therefore, develop similar to other vertebrate animals.

Compare the human embryo to the other vertebrate embryos in the pictures below. Identify and label the parts that are the same in each picture.

Human Embryo

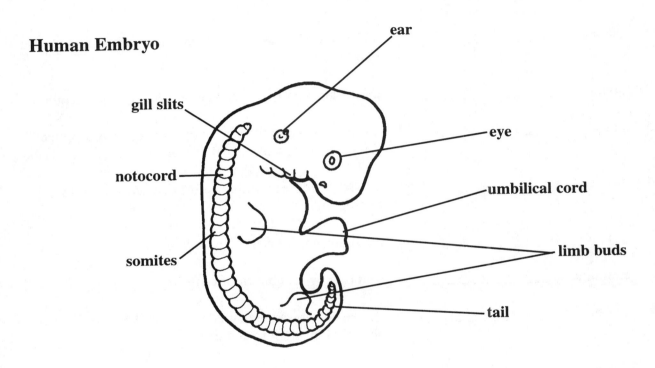

Reptile Embryo

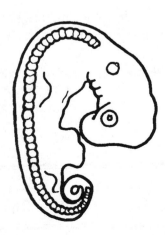

Bird Embryo

Fish Embryo

Dinosaur Defenses

Dinosaurs just like all other animals depend on plants and other animals for food. All dinosaurs had special characteristics that helped them survive.

Read the descriptions of Dino Defenses. Cut out the pictures of the dinosaurs at the bottom of the page and glue them in place to match the descriptions.

Dino Defenses

1. Hard, shell-like plates, much like a turtle shell, covered their body. Some had huge, bony club tails to swing and hit predators.	2. Long, sharp horns on its head and nose were lowered to face the enemy. A bony shield protected its neck from a predator's bite.	3. A thick, bone-like helmet, with sharp spikes sticking out, completely covered its head. It probably lowered its head and rammed the enemy as protection.
4. A sharp, spiked tail to swing in the direction of a predator and hard, bony plates running from head to tail helped to protect it from harm.	5. Six inch long, sharp teeth in a huge mouth and very sharp claws on hands and feet helped it hold and kill prey quickly.	6. The enormous size of the dinosaur along with its long, whip-like tail was enough to protect it against carnivores.

Tyrannosaurus   Ankylosaurus   Triceratops

Stegosaurus   Apatosaurus   Pachycephalosaurus

Feathered Reptiles

Because birds have some of the same characteristics as reptiles they are sometimes referred to as "feathered reptiles." Scientists believe that feathers replaced the scales of the small theropod dinosaurs and they slowly evolved into birds. Bird ancestors have been traced back through history to animals called "Archaeopteryx" (ar-kee-ahp-ter-ix) which probably looked like a small dinosaur with wings and feathers. This bird-reptile was about the size of a crow. It had hollow bones, a long beak and wings, and legs like a bird. The wings had long feathers that allowed it to glide through the air. Each wing had three long, clawed fingers attached that enabled it to climb trees like a small reptile. It had a long, thin, lizard-like tail with feathers running down each side. Unlike present-day birds, its long beak was full of teeth. Fossils of Archaeopteryx are considered to be the most valuable fossil in the world because they come from the oldest bird in history.

Read the information above again, paying special attention to the description of the bird-reptile called Archaeopteryx. Draw a picture in the box of the way you think this ancient bird looked.

Mass Extinction Mystery

The disappearance of the dinosaurs is still a mystery. Many theories as to why this happened are given below. Read each one. Which theory do you think is the real answer to the mysterious mass extinction of the dinosaurs? When you are through, write the cause-and-effect theory that you believe is the correct one. Justify your choice with at least three reasons.

Cause and Effect Theories of Extinction

Cause: A giant meteorite, 5 to 10 miles (8–16 km) wide and traveling at 50,000 miles per hour (85,000 kph) crashed into the Earth.

Effect: A column of dust was thrown into the stratosphere blocking the sun and causing plants and other food sources to disappear.

Cause: A supernova (star) exploded very near the Earth.

Effect: Extreme radiation covered the Earth for a period of 10–20 years, causing the plants and some animals to die.

Cause: Volcanic activity all over the Earth temporarily destroyed the Earth's ozone layer.

Effect: Too much ultraviolet radiation from the sun was allowed to reach the Earth, burning all exposed plant and animal life.

Cause: Volcanic activity on the sea floor forced the breakup of the continents and the shallow seas disappeared.

Effect: The land grew cold and animals without protective coverings, such as fur or feathers, could not survive.

My Opinion

Cause:

Effect:

_____

_____

_____

_____

Animal Time Line

Materials: *three 6' (1.8 m) pieces bulletin board paper*
pencils, markers, rulers, yardsticks, glue, crayons
copies of all animal pictures from Fingertip Facts (pages 67–77)
3 copies of reference charts (pages 61–66)

Directions: Divide students into three groups. Direct each group to measure and draw a line all the way across the long side of the paper, 5 inches (3 cm) down from the top. Then draw another line 5 inches (13 cm) below the first one. Give each group a copy of the reference charts. Assign each group a time era to complete using the reference charts as a guide. After the three sections are finished, have the students find the pictures of the animals listed on the reference charts. Color and glue them in the correct time periods. Hang the three sections end-to-end (Paleozoic - Mesozoic - Cenozoic) to complete the time line. Give each student a copy of the Time Line Questions to answer.

Follow the directions below for specific measurements on each chart.

Paleozoic Era:
Direct the students to measure across the paper and draw a line from top to bottom at each 10 inch (25 cm) intervals. There will be six sections 10 inches (25 cm) long and one section 12 inches (30 cm) long.

Mesozoic Era:
Direct students to measure across the paper and draw a line from top to bottom at each 2 foot (60 cm) interval. There will be three sections 2 feet (60 cm) long.

Cenozoic Era:
Direct the students to measure across the paper and draw a line from top to bottom at each 3 foot (.9 m) interval. There will be two sections 3 feet (90 cm) long.

← 6" →											
PALEOZOIC							**MESOZOIC**			**CENOZOIC**	
10"	10"	10"	10"	10"	10"	12"	2'	2'	2'	3'	3'

Animal Time Line (cont.)

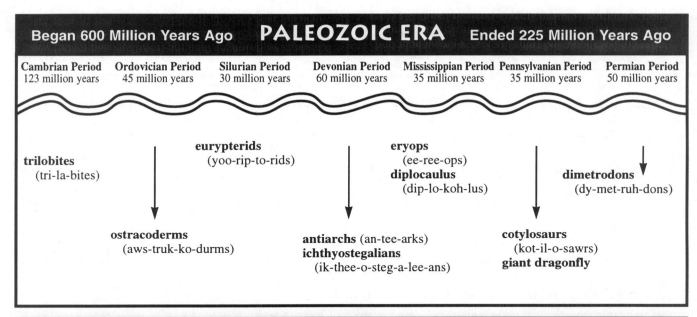

Began 600 Million Years Ago	PALEOZOIC ERA	Ended 225 Million Years Ago

Cambrian Period 123 million years	Ordovician Period 45 million years	Silurian Period 30 million years	Devonian Period 60 million years	Mississippian Period 35 million years	Pennsylvanian Period 35 million years	Permian Period 50 million years

trilobites
(tri-la-bites)

eurypterids
(yoo-rip-to-rids)

eryops
(ee-ree-ops)
diplocaulus
(dip-lo-koh-lus)

dimetrodons
(dy-met-ruh-dons)

ostracoderms
(aws-truk-ko-durms)

antiarchs (an-tee-arks)
ichthyostegalians
(ik-thee-o-steg-a-lee-ans)

cotylosaurs
(kot-il-o-sawrs)
giant dragonfly

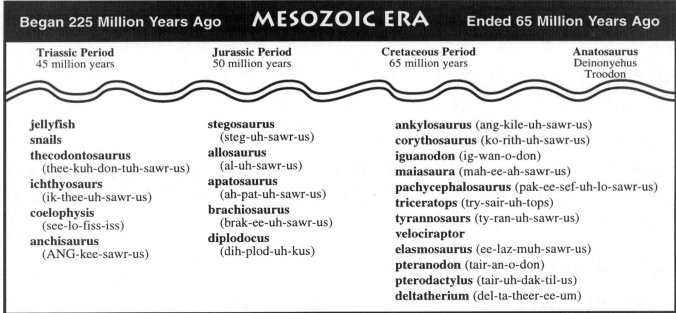

Began 225 Million Years Ago	MESOZOIC ERA	Ended 65 Million Years Ago

Triassic Period 45 million years	Jurassic Period 50 million years	Cretaceous Period 65 million years	Anatosaurus Deinonyehus Troodon

jellyfish
snails
thecodontosaurus
(thee-kuh-don-tuh-sawr-us)
ichthyosaurs
(ik-thee-uh-sawr-us)
coelophysis
(see-lo-fiss-iss)
anchisaurus
(ANG-kee-sawr-us)

stegosaurus
(steg-uh-sawr-us)
allosaurus
(al-uh-sawr-us)
apatosaurus
(ah-pat-uh-sawr-us)
brachiosaurus
(brak-ee-uh-sawr-us)
diplodocus
(dih-plod-uh-kus)

ankylosaurus (ang-kile-uh-sawr-us)
corythosaurus (ko-rith-uh-sawr-us)
iguanodon (ig-wan-o-don)
maiasaura (mah-ee-ah-sawr-us)
pachycephalosaurus (pak-ee-sef-uh-lo-sawr-us)
triceratops (try-sair-uh-tops)
tyrannosaurs (ty-ran-uh-sawr-us)
velociraptor
elasmosaurus (ee-laz-muh-sawr-us)
pteranodon (tair-an-o-don)
pterodactylus (tair-uh-dak-til-us)
deltatherium (del-ta-theer-ee-um)

Began 65 Million Years Ago	CENOZOIC ERA	Present Time

Tertiary Period 61.5 million years	Quaternary Period 3.5 million years

eohippus (ee-oh-hip-us)
smilodon (smy-luh-don)
diatryma (di-uh-try-ma)
wooly mammoth (wool-ee-mam-oth)
glyptodon (glip-toh-don)

mammals
birds
reptiles
fish
man

Time Line Questions

I. Use the Dinosaur Time Line to answer the following questions.

1. Name the three eras of time. _____

    _____

    _____

2. List the time periods in each of the three eras.

    Paleozoic: _____

    Mesozoic: _____

    Cenozoic: _____

3. Name the era and time period in which we now live. _____

    _____

    _____

4. What is the name of the time period from which the first fossils came? _____

    _____

    _____

5. What era of time is known as "The Age of the Dinosaur?" _____

    _____

    _____

6. In what time period did people first live on Earth? _____

    _____

    _____

7. Did dinosaurs live at the same time as people? _____

    _____

    _____

II If you could go back in time to one of the three eras, which one would you choose to visit? Write a story about your trip on another sheet of paper. Tell how you think the Earth looked, what kinds of plants and animals you would see, and where you might find shelter. Make up a title for your story.

Dinosaur Big Book

Materials:

> *12" x 18" (30 x 45 cm) white construction paper for book pages and title page*
> *12" x 18" (30 x 45 cm) colored construction paper for front and back cover*
> *9" x 12" (23 x 30 cm) construction paper*
> *wide-lined writing paper for text*
> *thin line markers for text*
> *crayons, markers, and water colors*
> *glue and scissors*

Procedure: Each student will have a page in the book to complete. More than one book can be made if the completed book will be too thick for all the pages. Direct each student to choose his or her favorite dinosaur. The students will use watercolors to paint the background on their page. While the background is drying, have them draw a picture of the dinosaur on a 9" x 12" (23 x 30 cm) piece of construction paper, decorate it with crayons and markers, cut it out and glue it at the bottom of the background page when it is dry. Next, each student will write their own story or copy the patterned writing on page 52 on writing paper with a thin marker and fill in the blanks with words that relate to his or her dinosaur picture. The students can use their dinosaur reports for reference books. Make the title page like the example below and let all the students sign it that have written a page in the book. They may decorate the covers any way they choose with cutouts, watercolors, crayons, or markers. After the book is finished, number and laminate all the parts. Bind the book on the side with tape, notebook rings, or yarn laced through holes.

Title Page

> _____
> *Title*
>
> ***Written and Illustrated by***
>
> _____
>
> _____
>
> _____
>
> ***Published by***
>
> _____
> *Teacher's Name and Room Number*

Patterned Writing

Patterned Writing

This is my favorite dinosaur. It is a (_____). It is classified as
name of dinosaur

(_____) dinosaur and its subgroup name is (_____). My favorite
an orithischian, a saurischian   *subgroup name*

dinosaur is (_____) because it eats (_____). It is
a carnivore, a herbivore, or an omnivore   *meat and/or plants*

(_____) because it walks on (_____). I like this dinosaur because
name of quadrupedal, bipedal   *two, four feet*

(_____).
three reasons

52

Explore the World Wide Web

The World Wide Web (WWW) is like a giant spider's web, only the threads are electronic lines of communication that stretch out over the entire Earth.

Millions of people explore the Web everyday. The trick is to find information and sites that you can use. Web Browsers, easy-to-use software programs, require a URL (address), typed exactly as it appears, to access information on a specific topic. A search engine can hunt down information on a specific subject and give you a matching list of sites.

Explore the WWW dinosaur sites available on the web using the URL addresses below or access a search engine and then type **dinosaurs** to view a list of sites to choose from. Many of the sites have pictures and sounds that can be downloaded for use in classrooms.

*****Note:** At the time of this printing all Web sites were accurate and accessible. The publishers give no guarantee as to how long these Web sites will remain online.

Dinosaur Sites

Dinosaur Literature Connections
> Children will be invited to choose a dinosaur to do an in depth research.
> http://www.coe.ufl.edu/faculty/lamme/project/dinosaurs/litdinosaurs.htlm

A to Z Science and Learning Store–Dinosaurs
> Learn about the lost world of dinosaurs. See our dino egg hatch. Links to the best dino web sites.
> http://www.a-two-z.com/page_d.html

Dinosaurs
> Tour of exhibits on dinosaurs.
> http://www.ucmpl.berkley.edu/exhibittext/cladecham.html

The Field Museum of Natural History
> Exhibits of dinosaurs and fossils.
> http://www.bvis.uic.edu:80/museum

DNA to Dinosaurs
> Fun, educational site about dinosaurs.
> http://www.bvis.uic.edu/museum/exhibits/Exhibits.html

Popular Search Engines

Yahoo! (http://www.yahoo.com)

Lycros (http://www.lycros.com)

Alta Vista (http://www.altavista.digital.com)

*****Note:** At the time of this printing all Web sites were accurate and accessible. The publishers give no guarantee as to how long these Web sites will remain online.

What if...?

Creative Writing Topics

Listed below are suggestions for using the creative writing topics.

1. Select one topic per day, discuss and expand the topic, and then have students write in their journals for a specified amount of time.

2. Present students with several topics from which to choose.

3. Provide students with a copy of all the topics for homework; determine a due date for each one.

4. Cut apart the rectangles, place them in a bag, and let each student draw one.

5. Let the students draw one topic from the Creative Writing envelope on the "What Am I?" bulletin board when they have free time.

What if humans become extinct like the dinosaurs? What species would take the place of humans?
What if you were the last human on Earth? Where would you live? Would you be happy all alone on Earth?
What if dinosaurs were still alive and could talk? What would you say to a dinosaur?
What if you found the fossil of a dinosaur? How would you get the fossil out of the rock without destroying it?
What if you found a dinosaur egg? What if it hatched and thought you were its mother or daddy? How would you take care of a baby dinosaur?
What if you were sent back in time to the age of the dinosaurs? Where would you live? What would you eat? What would you wear?
What if you could ride on a flying dinosaur? Where would you go? What would you see?
What if you could see a dinosaur that no one else could see? How could you make it visible to everyone else?
What if you were in a museum and a huge dinosaur skeleton fell apart after you touched it? How would you explain what happened?
What if you were suddenly changed into a dinosaur? What would you think about? Who would you play with and talk to?
What if you lived near a volcano and it started to erupt? Where would you go to get away from the hot lava and ash?
What if you found a cave that went deep down into the Earth and got lost when you went inside? How would you find your way out?
What if you were on a trip in the mountains and found a lost city? What kind of people and animals would you find?
What if animals ruled the Earth and humans were their pets? What kind of animal would you want to belong to and why?

54

Dinosaur Poetry

From the Works of Jack Prelutsky

Tyrannosaurs Was a Beast contains different poems about dinosaurs. Each poem provides the correct pronunciation for the dinosaur's name, describes the dinosaur, and discusses its characteristics in rhyme. Illustrated by Arnold Lobel, the pictures present the dinosaurs in the same whimsical way described by Jack Prelutsky. These poems can be used to introduce the different dinosaurs and their characteristics to children.

Something Big Has Been Here contains two poetry selections that are appropriate for this unit. The poem "Something Big Has Been Here" could lead to an illustration and description of the very large "Something" that made the footprint. "I Saw a Brontosaurus" is a favorite of all children. The descriptive language in this poem can be used to teach the meaning of new vocabulary through the use of synonyms. After reading the poem through once, a thesaurus can be used to rewrite each line using synonyms in place of unfamiliar words, to help children understand the selection better. "I Saw A Brontosaurus" can also be used to produce a student book illustrating the story in the poem.

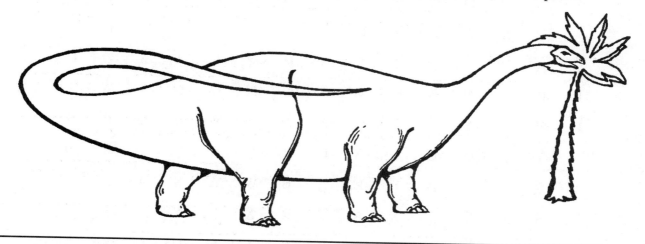

From the Works of Shel Silverstein

"Prehistoric," from *A Light in the Attic*, gives an entertaining account of all kinds of prehistoric animals and Silverstein's explanation of their evolution into the animals on earth today. The poem could be used as an introduction to the Animal Time Line.

Where the Sidewalk Ends contains a short, amusing poem about naming a dinosaur. "If I Had a Brontosaurus" could lead into a discussion on the differences between male and female animals/dinosaurs and comparisons of animal/dinosaur reproduction.

Activity: Make a Dinosaur Poetry Book

Have each student write his or her own dinosaur poems and compile them into a dinosaur poetry book. They may illustrate them or use pictures found in Fingertip Facts on pages 60–77. Direct them to create a table of contents and covers for their books.

Dinosaur Word Search

```
F  A  D  I  M  E  T  R  O  D  O  N  T  A  B
T  R  I  C  E  R  A  T  O  P  S  B  R  B  R
Y  S  P  S  P  I  N  O  S  A  U  R  U  S  S
R  U  L  I  T  A  P  A  U  C  D  A  A  I  A
A  R  O  G  E  T  N  N  R  F  E  N  S  C  C
N  U  D  U  R  R  O  K  U  A  N  K  L  O  S
N  A  O  A  A  A  U  Y  A  G  H  Y  S  D  H
O  S  C  N  N  K  G  L  S  P  R  L  U  I  S
S  O  U  O  O  H  I  T  O  H  U  O  R  P  U
A  C  S  D  D  J  U  L  I  L  A  S  U  L  R
U  A  K  O  O  I  E  S  H  M  S  A  A  O  U
R  R  T  N  N  O  M  A  C  N  O  U  S  A  A
U  Y  A  Y  C  P  G  R  A  V  M  R  O  R  S
S  T  E  G  O  S  A  U  R  U  S  U  T  C  O
Y  S  A  O  A  F  L  A  B  W  A  S  A  A  L
T  S  U  T  E  X  A  T  R  X  L  Y  P  E  L
D  I  N  O  S  A  U  R  S  T  E  U  A  K  A
```

These animals are all extinct. Find their names in the puzzle above.

Tyrannosaurs	Styracosuarus	Diplodocus
Iguanodon	Pteranodon	Brachiosaurus
Elasmosaur	Ankylosaurus	Allosaurus
Stegosaurus	Dinosaurs	Spinosaurus
Triceratops	Apatosaurus	Dimetrodon

Animal Web of Life

Every plant and animal on Earth is an important part of nature's Web of Life. A Web of Life is made of many individual food chains. Plants and animals are all links in a food chain that begins, ends, and begins again with the sun. Through a process of eating and being eaten, energy supplied by the sun, passes from plants to herbivores, to carnivores and omnivores, to decomposers and then begins again as new plants grow in the soil.

Materials:

Small pictures or written names of plants and animals from the groups listed with the colors below. (Pictures are not needed for the sun and soil.)

Construction paper cut in 2 inch strips to represent the following groups:

> *yellow* – sun
> *green* – plants
> *blue* – omnivores
> *orange* – herbivores
> *red* – carnivores
> *purple* – detritivores (decomposers)
> *brown* – soil

- Have the students make a large paper chain circle, with two links for each student in the classroom, to represent the sun.

- Give each student a strip from each of the other color groups.

- Have each student select a picture or name from the green, blue, orange, red, and purple groups above and glue them onto the correct color strip. Then have them glue the strips together in the order above with green first and brown last. (Note: The blue omnivore strip can be placed anywhere in the chain between the green and purple strips.)

- Give each student two yellow strips and have them join both ends of their chain to two links in the chain representing the sun.

- To help students understand the importance of each link in the food chain brainstorm what would happen if a link in the chain is broken.

- Hang the Web of Life in the classroom after it is complete.

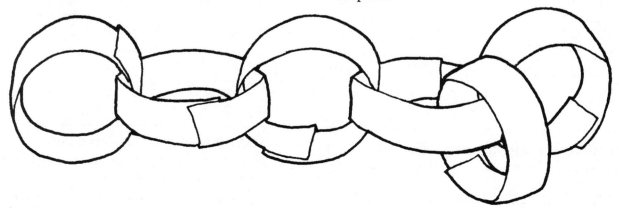

Plant Pollination

Fossils of flowering plants that the dinosaurs fed on probably had a single stem with hundreds of flower blossoms. Bee-like insects that developed during the Mesozoic Era helped pollinate these flowers just as honeybees pollinate 85% of crops today.

Using the frames below, read and then illustrate the story of honeybees and pollination.

How Honeybees Help Pollinate Flowering Plants

A worker honeybee leaves the bee hive to search for pollen. Honeybees need pollen to make honey.	He flies to a flower and collects tiny pollen grains from the flower's stamen. He carries the pollen in a special "basket" on his hind leg.

He flies to another flower. Some of the pollen grains shake off and fall on the stigma to the flower.	The honeybee carries the rest of the pollen grains back to the hive to feed the young honeybees and the queen.

The flower begins to make a seed that will eventually grow into a new flower.	Many flowering plants depend on the small honeybee to help them transfer pollen so that new plants can grow.

58

Paper Plate Dinosaur

Materials: paper plates, scissors, crayons or markers, paper fastener, hold punch, copy of dinosaur pattern for each child

Procedure: Cut a paper plate in half. Cut out pieces and decorate. Attach head, legs, and tail as illustrated.

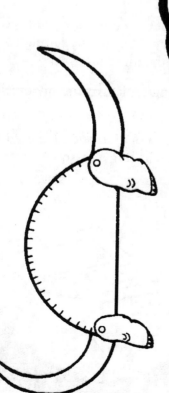

Using Fingertip Facts

Fingertip Facts are designed to serve as a resource and quick reference about dinosaurs. They are divided into two groups, information cards and picture cards. These cards will teach you about dinosaurs, plants, and other inhabitants of the earth in different geological eras.

The unit provides many ways to use the Fingertip Facts. Several other ways to use these handy fact cards are listed below.

- Reproduce these pages. Put the picture and the fact cards together. Bind into a book for a Dinosaur Fact Book. Let students color the pictures.

- Make dinosaur flash cards. Cut out the cards and glue them onto index cards. Use the flash cards to play a matching game. Have students match the picture to the information.

- Enlarge any of the pictures. This can be done on a copy machine that has this function or by using an opaque projector. To do this, attach a large piece of paper on the wall. Project the picture onto the paper and use a pencil or marker to outline. Adjust the image to the size you want the final product to be. The pictures can be used for bulletin boards, shape books, notebook covers, or any place you want a little dinosaur decoration.

- Use the page to let students create little books. For younger children or to save time, reproduce the pages and the text, and put them in an order that you choose. This can be by largest to smallest dinosaur, one time period to another, or alphabetical order. Older students can make their own books, using the information from the cards to write their own text.

- Let students choose a dinosaur to write a report about by cutting up the pictures, placing them in a bag or box, and letting them choose their subjects randomly.

- Play a guessing game. Choose an information card. Give clues about the dinosaur you have chosen and have the students guess which dinosaur you are describing. Vary the game by letting the students choose the correct picture rather than just say the name of the dinosaur.

- Use the shapes to make flash cards on which to write creative writing topics, or for any other use that might reinforce basic skills.

- Create a Fingertip Fact File. Reproduce the cards onto index paper or cut out and glue onto index cards. Laminate. Place in a file or shoe box. Refer to cards when teaching a lesson, or let student use them for reference.

Fingertip Facts

Parasaurolophus *(par-ah-sawr-OL-uh-fus)*

Geological Time: Mesozoic Era/Late Cretaceous Period

Dinosaur Group: Ornithischian	**Height:**	16 feet (4.8 m)
Classification: Ornithopoda	**Weight:**	3 to 4 tons (2.7 - 3.6 met. tons)
Features: Herbivore Bipedal	**Length:**	30 feet (9 m)

Fossils found in: North America, Asia, Europe, Canada

Parasaurolophus was a duck-billed dinosaur with a 5 foot (1.5 m) long, hollow, pointed crest on top of its head. It walked upright on its two hind legs with its tail held high for balance. Its hands and three-toed feet were webbed. Parasaurolophus' crest was similar to several other dinosaurs, so it was given the name "similar-crested lizard."

Pachycephalosaurus *(pak-ee-SEF-uh-lo-sawr-us)*

Geological Time: Mesozoic Era/Late Cretaceous Period

Dinosaur Group: Ornithischian	**Height:**	10-15 feet (3 - 4.5 m)
Classification: Pachy-cephalosaur	**Weight:**	100-500 lbs. (45 - 225 kg)
Features: Herbivore Bipedal	**Length:**	15 feet (4.5 m)

Fossils found in: North America, China, England, Mongolia

Pachycephalosaurus had a bony, dome-shaped head that was 9 inches (23 cm) thick. Because of its thick skull it was named "thick-headed lizard." Bony knobs were all over its head and short, sharp spikes stuck out from its nose. Pachycephalosaurus was the only ornithischian without a beaked face.

Stegosaurus *(STEG-uh-sawr-us)*

Geological Time: Mesozoic Era/Late Jurassic Period

Dinosaur Group: Ornithischian	**Height:**	16 feet (4.8 m)
Classification: Stegosaur	**Weight:**	2 to 3 tons (1.8 - 2.7 met. tons)
Features: Herbivore Quadrupedal	**Length:**	25 feet (7.5 m)

Fossils found in: North America, Europe

Stegosaurus is known as the "plated lizard" because of the two rows of leaf-shaped, bony plates extending from behind the head to the middle of the tail. Scientists believe that the plates may have been used to help keep Stegosaurus cool. Its long, heavy tail had four sharp spikes. Stegosaurus' hind legs were longer than its front legs making its small head very low to the ground.

Cycad Tree *(Sy-kad)*

The cycad tree is a large, tropical, cone-bearing seed plant. It is the most primitive seed plant known. It was very common during the time of the dinosaurs but it grows only in a few small areas today. Its leafy fern-like branches grow in a circular pattern around its large seed cones. It grows to a height of 60 feet (18 m) and has leaves only at the top.

Ornithischian Dinosaurs (or-ni-THISS-kee-an)

Geological Time: Triassic through Cretaceous

Ornithischian dinosaurs had hipbones that resembled the hipbones of present-day birds. All of these dinosaurs ere herbivores (plant eaters), all had hoofed toes and all, except one, Pachycephalosaurus (pak-ee-sef-uh-lo-sawr-us) had a beak-like mouth. Some dinosaurs of this kind were bipedal; others were quadrupedal. They lived all over the world during the Triassic Period and died out in the late Cretaceous Period after roaming the earth for 150 million years.

Ornithischian dinosaurs include the subgroup classifications of:

Ornithopoda
(bird-footed reptiles)
Corythosaurus
Iguanodon
Parasaurolophus

Stegosaur
(plated reptiles)
Stegosaurus

Pachycephalosaur
(thick-headed reptiles)
Pachycephalosaurus

Ceratopsia
(horned-faced reptiles)
Triceratops
Styracosaurus

Ankylosaur
(armor covered reptile)
Ankylosaurus

Fingertip Facts *(cont.)*

Saurischian Dinosaurs *(sawr-ISS-kee-uhn)*

Geological Time: Triassic through Cretaceous

Saurischian dinosaurs had hipbones that resembled the hips of present-day lizards. All of this group had clawed feet. The smallest and largest dinosaurs known were members of this group. Saurischian dinosaurs included herbivores and carnivores. Some were bipedal with short arms while others were quadrupedal. They lived all over the world for 150 million years, from the middle of the Triassic Period until the end of the Cretaceous Period.

Saurischian dinosaurs include the subgroup classifications of:

Theropoda *(beast-footed reptiles)*	**Sauropoda** *(lizard-footed reptiles)*
Allosaurus	Apatosaurus
Coelophysis	Brachiosaurus
Spinosaurus	Diplodocus
Tyrannosaurs	

Pteranodon *(tair-AN-o-don)*

Geological Time: Mesozoic Era/Late Cretaceous Period
Group: Flying Reptile
Classification: Pterosaur **Weight:** 30 - 40 pounds (13 - 18 kg)
Features: Carnivore Bipedal/Winged
Length: 6 feet (2m)
Fossils found: All over the world

Pteranodon was a flying reptile with a wing spread of 27 feet (8.1 m). Its head and crest were 6 feet (2 m) long and its bird-like beak did not have teeth. This bird-like reptile glided through the air rather than flying and it may have been covered in fur. Its name means "winged and toothless" because it could fly and did not have teeth.

Ankylosaurus *(ang-KILE-uh-sawr-us)*

Geological Time: Mesozoic Era/Cretaceous Period
Dinosaur Group: Ornithischian
Height: 4 feet (1.2 m)
Classification: Ankylosaur
Weight: 5 tons (4.5 met. tons)
Features: Herbivore Quadruped
Length: 25 feet (7.5 m)
Fossils found in: North America, Europe, Asia, Australia

Ankylosaurus was known as "stiffened lizard" because it was covered with a bony, shell-like covering. It had a triangle-shaped head, a 6 foot (1.8 m) wide body with a row of short, sharp spikes on its sides and back, and a thick, bony club at the end of its tail.

Corythosaurus *(ko-RITH-uh-sawr-us)*

Geological Time: Mesozoic Era/Late Cretaceous Period
Dinosaur Group: Ornithischian
Height: 15 - 20 feet (4.5 - 6 m)
Classification: Ornithopoda
Weight: 2 to 3 tons (1.8 - 2.7 met. tons)
Features: Herbivore Bipedal
Length: 30 feet (9 m)
Fossils found in: Canada

Corythosaurus had a hollow, helmet-shaped crest on its head. It had a duck-billed head and webbed feet. It walked on two feet with its long tail held straight behind for balance. Corythosaurus was known as "helmet lizard" because of the crest on its head.

Iguanodon *(ig-WAN-o-don)*

Geological Time: Mesozoic Era/Early Cretaceous Period
Dinosaur Group: Ornithischian
Height: 15 feet (4.5 m)
Classification: Ornithopoda
Weight: 5 tons (4.5 met. tons)
Features: Herbivore Bipedal
Length: 25 feet (7.5 m)
Fossils found in: North America, South America, Asia, Australia

Iguanodon was the first dinosaur fossil ever found. It walked upright on its two strong, hind legs; each foot had three toes. Its short arms had four fingers and one sharp, pointed, spike-like thumb on each hand. Iguanodon was named "Iguana-tooth" because its teeth were like the nose of the iguana lizard.

Fingertip Facts *(cont.)*

Mesozoic Era *(mez-uh-ZO-ik)*

The Mesozoic Era of time is known as the "Age of the Reptiles" or the "Age of the Dinosaurs" because huge reptiles known as dinosaurs roamed the earth in great numbers. The Mesozoic Era came between the Paleozoic Era and the Cenozoic Era and means "middle time." It began 225 million years ago and ended 65 million years ago. It is divided into three separate time periods: the Triassic, the Jurassic, and the Cretaceous. When the Mesozoic Era ended, all of the dinosaurs had disappeared from earth.

Diplodocus *(dih-PLOD-uh-kus)*

Geological Time:	Mesozoic Era/Late Jurassic Period		
Dinosaur Group:	Saurischia	**Height:**	25 feet (7.5 m)
Classification:	Sauropoda	**Weight:**	25 tons (22 met. tons)
Features:	Herbivore Quadrupedal	**Length:**	90 feet (927 m)
Fossils found in:	North America, Asia, Europe, Africa		

Diplodocus was the longest dinosaur. It had a 26 foot (8 m) long neck, small head, long, heavy body and a 45 foot (13 m) long tail. It had longer back legs than front legs and huge, heavy feet. Diplodocus had a long, whip-like tail and "Y-shaped" vertebrae that made it possible for it to move from side to side and used it as a weapon. It was named "double-beamed" because of its unusually shaped vertebrae.

Spinosaurus *(Spy-nuh-sawr-us)*

Geological Time:	Mesozoic Era/Late Cretaceous Period		
Dinosaur Group:	Saurischian	**Height:**	15 feet (4.5 m)
Classification:	Theropoda	**Weight:**	3 - 4 tons (2.7 - 3.6 met. tons)
Features:	Carnivore Bipedal	**Length:**	40 feet (12 m)
Fossils found in:	North Africa		

Spinosaurus had 6 foot (2 m) tall spines running the length of its back. The spines held a sail that started just below the neck and extended down the back to below the hips. Its arms were short and its feet and hands had long sharp claws. Because of the spiny sail it was named "spiny lizard."

Tyrannosaurs *(ty-RAN-uh-sawr-us)*

Geological Time:	Mesozoic Era/Late Cretaceous Period		
Dinosaur Group:	Saurischian	**Height:**	18 - 20 feet (6 m)
Classification:	Theropoda	**Weight:**	6 tons (5.4 met. tons)
Features:	Carnivore Bipedal	**Length:**	50 feet long (15 m)
Fossils found in:	North America, Mongolia, India, Japan		

Tyrannosaurs was the largest and last of the meat-eating dinosaurs. Its massive, 6 foot long (2 m) head held long, razor-sharp teeth. It had huge hind legs, large feet, and short arms. Each three-toed foot and three-fingered hand was equipped with long, sharp claws. Tyrannosaurs was give the name "tyrant lizard" because of its extremely sharp claws and teeth.

Palm Tree

The Palm Tree grows best on sandy beaches in tropical weather. It is an evergreen tree with leaves that are 12 to 15 feet (about 4 m) long. The leaves grow like a head at the top of the stalk. The palm tree grows 30 to 50 feet (9 - 15 m) tall.

Apatosaurus/Brontosaurus
(uh-PAH-toh-sawr-us/BRAHN-toh-sawr-us)

Geological Time:	Mesozoic Era/Late Jurassic Period		
Dinosaur Group:	Saurischian	**Height:**	35 feet (10 m)
Classification:	Sauropoda	**Weight:**	30 tons (27 met. tons)
Features:	Herbivore Quadrupedal	**Length:**	75 feet (23 m)
Fossils found in:	North America, Europe		

Apatosaurus was one of the largest sauropod dinosaurs. Its enormous body weighed 60 thousand pounds (27 thousand kg). It had a small head, a 20 foot (6 m) long neck, a long, thick tail and large, heavy legs. Its front legs were shorter than the back legs. Apatosaurus is sometimes called Brontosaurus, and because it is sometimes confused with other dinosaurs of this group, it was named "deceptive lizard."

Fingertip Facts *(cont.)*

Brachiosaurus *(BRAK-ee-uh-sawr-us)*

Geological Time: Mesozoic Era/Jurassic Period
Dinosaur Group: Saurischian **Height:** 45 feet (13.5 m)
Classification: Sauropoda **Weight:** 70 to 80 tons (63 - 72 met. tons)
Features: Herbivore Quadrupedal **Length:** 85 feet (26 m)
Fossils found in: North America, Africa, Europe

Brachiosaurus is the largest known land animal. Its heavy body was larger than any other dinosaur from the Sauropoda group. Its neck was almost 30 feet (9 m) long but its tail was short. It had huge elephant-like feet and its front legs were longer than its back legs. It was known as "arm lizard" because of the longer front legs.

Coelophysis *(see-lo-FIS-iss)*

Geological Time: Mesozoic Era/Triassic Period
Dinosaur Group: Saurischian **Height:** 5 feet (1.5 m)
Classification: Theropoda **Weight:** 100 pounds (45 kg)
Features: Carnivore Bipedal **Length:** 10 feet (3 m)
Fossils found in: North America, Germany

Coelophysis was a small two-legged meat eater. It had a small head with long jaws and sharp teeth. Its neck and tail were both long and thin. Its legs were slender and each of its three toes had sharp claws. Its arms were short with three, clawed fingers on each hand. Its name means "hollow form" because of the hollow bones inside its body. Because it was capable of running very fast, some scientists believe that Coelophysis was a warm-blooded animal that gave birth to live young rather than laying eggs.

Redwood Tree

The redwood tree is one of the tallest conifer trees still in existence. It grows to a height of 200 to 300 feet (60 - 90 m) It is a cone-bearing tree with needle-like leaves. Moist steam banks and slopes offer it the best habitat.

Styracosaurus *(sty-RAK-uh-sawr-us)*

Geological Time: Mesozoic Era/Late Cretaceous Period
Dinosaur Group: Ornithischian **Height:** 6 feet (1.8 m)
Classification: Herbivore Quadrupedal **Length:** 18 feet (5.5 m)
Fossils found in: North America, Mongolia

Styracosaurus had a large, heavy body, thick legs, and a short tail. The back legs were longer than the front legs. It was given the name "spiked lizard" because the frill, extending back over its shoulders, had six long, sharp spikes around the edge. There was one long, sharp horn at the end of its nose.

Triceratops *(try-SAIR-uh-tops)*

Geological Time: Mesozoic Era/Late Cretaceous Period
Dinosaur Group: Ornithischian **Height:** 9 feet (2.7 m)
Classification: Ceratopsia **Weight:** 5 tons (4.5 met. tons)
Features: Herbivore Quadrupedal **Length:** 25 feet (7.5 m)
Fossils found in: North America, Mongolia

Triceratops was the largest and heaviest of the ceratopsian dinosaurs. It was named "three-horned face" because there were two short, sharp horns over each eye and one longer horn on its nose. Its legs were thick, the hind legs were longer than the front legs and its tail was short and heavy. Its head held a smooth, round frill that extended back over its shoulders.

Kelp

The common name for brown algae (seaweed) is kelp. The kelp plant grows in shallow water along cooler coastlines. They can grow to immense size, 98 feet long, are known for their rapid growth. Kelp contains many vitamins and minerals and were probably a major food source for dinosaurs.

Horsetail

The horsetail is a non-flowering plant that has very narrow leaves an a jointed stem. It is sometimes referred to as equisetum plant.

64

Fingertip Facts *(cont.)*

Allosaurus *(al-uh-sawr-us)*

Geological Time: Mesozoic Era/Jurassic Period

Dinosaur Group: Saurischian **Height:** 16 feet (4.8 m)

Classification: Theropoda **Weight:** 4 tons (3.6 met. tons)

Features: Carnivore **Length:** 35 - 40 feet
Bipedal (11 - 12 m)

Fossils found in: North America, Africa and Asia

Allosaurus was one of the largest meat eating dinosaurs of the Jurassic time period. It walked upright on two strong, hind legs with its tail stretched out behind for balance. Its three-toed feet and three-fingered hands were armed with long claws. Allosaurus was named "different lizard" because the vertebrae in its backbone were arranged differently than any other lizard known.

Ginkgo Tree *(gen-ko)*

The ginkgo tree was once thought to be an extinct species but was found growing in the temple gardens of China and Japan. It is native only to Oriental regions but is found all over the world in present-day. The ginkgo tree's broad, fan-shaped leaves are dark green and it bears a yellow fruit.

Dimetrodon *(dy-MET-ruh-don)*

Geological Time: Paleozoic Era/Permian Period

Group: Mammal-like **Height:** 5 - 6 feet
Reptile including sail (1.5 - 2 m)

Classification: Pelycosaur

Features: Carnivore **Length:** 10 feet
Quadrupedal (3 m)

Fossils found in: North America

Dimetrodon was a meat-eating ancestor of early reptiles. It looked somewhat like an alligator of present-day. Its legs sprawled out from under its long, heavy body. A four foot (1 m) sail ran from behind the shoulder to the beginning of the tail. Its strong jaws held two different-sized teeth, and for that reason it was given the name "two-measure teeth."

Elasmosaurus *(ee-LAZ-muh-sawr-us)*

Geological Time: Mesozoic Era/Late Cretaceous Period

Group: Marine Reptile

Classification: Plesiosaur

Features: Carnivore **Length:** 43 feet
Quadrupedal (flippers) (13 m)

Fossils found on: Every Continent

Elasmosaurus was a marine reptile that swam the warm oceans during the same time period as the dinosaurs. Elasmosaurus had a long, thin neck, a short tail and body, and flippers shaped like paddles. Some scientists believe the Elasmosaurus could leave the water and move around on land as walruses do today. It was named "thin-plated lizard" because it had plate-like bones in its pelvis.

Pterodactylus *(tair-uh-DAK-til-us)*

Geological Time: Mesozoic Era/Late Jurassic Period

Group: Flying Reptile

Classification: Pterosaur **Weight:** 1–10 pounds (1 - 5 kg)

Features: Carnivore **Length:** 6 - 24 inches
Bipedal/Winged (15 - 60 cm)

Fossils found in: Europe, Africa

Pterodactylus was a small flying reptile with small bristle-like teeth. Some were smaller than sparrows and others as large as hawks. It was named "winged finger" because the fourth finger of each hand held the wing. It had a wide wingspan and glided through the air instead of flying. Its legs and feet were well suited to walking on land and it probably spent more time on the ground than in the air. Pterodactylus had no crest on its head.

Fern

The Fern is a low growing plant that was abundant in prehistoric eras and is still plentiful today. It has lacy, green leaves, called fronds, and long thin stalks. Ferns are very hardy and live in almost every climate and habitat.

Algae

Algae is a plant that is capable of living in almost any habitat where there is sunlight and water. Some visible signs of algae growth are discoloration on the side of aquarium glass, pond scum, and seaweed. Rapid population growth of red algae (red tide) can produce toxins which cause sickness and death of marine wildlife when it invades coastlines.

Fingertip Facts *(cont.)*

Anatosaurus *(an-NAT-uh-sawr-us)*

Geological Time: Late Cretaceous

Dinosaur Group:	Ornithischian	**Height:**	14 feet (4.3 m)
Classification:	Ornithopoda	**Weight:**	3.5 tons (3.2 met. tons)
Features:	Herbivore Bipedal	**Length:**	30 feet (9 m)

Fossils found in: North America and England

Many fossils and skin impressions of this duck-bill dinosaur have been found. It is one of the best known dinosaurs. It had skin the texture of rough stones. Its diet consisted of shrubs, seeds, evergreen needles, and fruits. It had a flat head, duck-bill and as many as 1000 teeth. Although it's forefeet were webbed feet the Anatosaurus was a land dweller.

Anchisaurus *(ANG-kee-sawr-us)*

Geological Time: Late Triassic and Early Jurassic

Dinosaur Group:	Saurischian	**Height:**	8 feet (2.5 m)
Classification:	Prosauropoda		
Features:	Omnivore Quadruped	**Length:**	12 feet (3.5 m)

Fossils found in: North America, United States, South Africa, and Germany

This is a very early dinosaur that resembled a reptile but with smaller feet and head. Although it was quadrupedal it could stand and run swiftly on two feet. It had sharp serrated teeth but ate plants as well as meat.

Deinonychus *(dyne-ON-ik-us)*

Geological Time: Early Cretaceous

Dinosaur Group:	Saurischian	**Height:**	5 feet (1.5 m)
Classification:	Theropoda	**Weight:**	175 pounds (80 kg)
Features:	Carnivore Bipedal	**Length:**	9 feet (2.7 m)

Fossils found in: United States

Deinonychus is one of the small theropod dinosaurs that had hind legs that were built especially for speed and savage attack. It had a short neck, large head filled with sharp, serrated teeth and excellent eyesight. Each foot had a sickle-shaped retractable claw that could be used to slash open the bellies of prey. Because Deinonychus hunted in packs of three or more, it could attack animals much larger than itself.

Maiasaura *(mah-ee-ah-SAWR-uh)*

Geological Time: Late Cretaceous

Dinosaur Group:	Ornithischian	**Height:**	15 feet (4.5 m)
Classification:	Ornithopoda		
Features:	Herbivore Bipedal	**Length:**	30 feet (9 m)

Fossils found in: United States

Maiasaura was named "good mother lizard" because it was found near a nest of 15 maiasaura babies. The only fossil of this dinosaur, a skull, shows it had a tiny horn-shaped crest between it's eyes. The baby fossils were 3 feet (1 m) long and 123 inches (30 cm) tall. There were many other dinosaur nests in the same area giving some evidence that these dinosaurs cared for their babies.

Troodon *(TROO-o-don)*

Geological Time: Cretaceous

Dinosaur Group: Ornithischian

Classification: Ornithopoda

Features: Carnivore, Bipedal

Fossils found in: United States

Troodon was a small carnivorous dinosaur named for the shape of its teeth (wound teeth) which were long and slender in front and blade-shaped and serrated in the back. There has been some disagreement on whether this dinosaur should be classified as an Ornithischian, ornithopoda instead of a theropod. If it remains classified as above it will be the only know flesh eating dinosaur in the Onithischian group.

Velociraptor *(veh-loss-ih-RAP-tor)*

Geological Time: Late Cretaceous

Dinosaur Group:	Saurischia	**Height:**	6 to 7 feet

Classification: Theropoda

Features: Carnivore, Bipedal

Fossils found in: Mongolia

Velociraptor resembled Deinonychus and was just as deadly. Its small slender body and strong legs were built for running. It had small, three fingered hands and a sharp, curved claw on each foot. One of the fossils found in Mongolia was still gripping the skull of a Protoceratops and the curved claw was still imbedded in the stomach of the other animal. Velociraptor was about as tall as a man and probably hunted in packs.

Fingertip Facts *(cont.)*

Trilobite *(tri-la-bite)*

Trilobites were flat shellfish with no backbones.

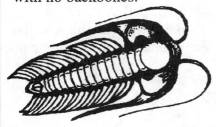

Jellyfish

Snail

Ostracoderm *(as-stra-ka-duarm)*

Ostracoderm looked like fish but only had a small hole for a mouth.

Eurypterid *(yoo-rip-to-rid)*

Eurypterids resembled spiders or crabs but grew to be six feet long.

Antiarch *(an-tee-ark)*

Antiarch were the first fish with mouths. They had a bony armor over their body instead of scales.

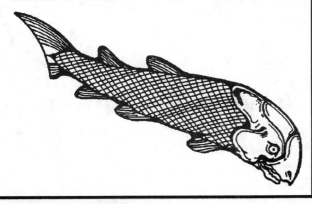

Ichthyostegalian
(ik-thee-ah-steg-ay-lee-an)

Ichthyostegalians are the earliest known amphibians. They had tails like fish but had legs instead of fins.

Fingertip Facts *(cont.)*

Eryops

Eryops and diplocaulus are examples of later amphibians with long tails and legs but no fins.

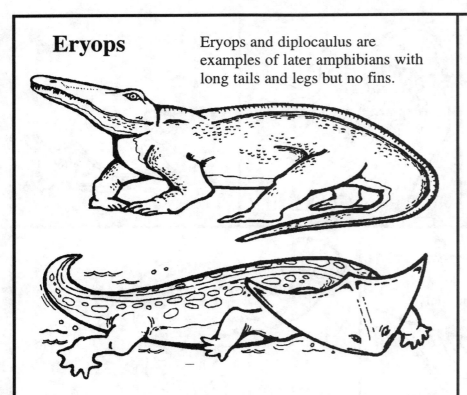

Giant Dragonfly

The giant dragonfly had a wingspread of over two feet (61 cm). All invertebrate animals grew very large in the early time periods before man.

Cotylosaur *(kaht-il-o-sawr)*

Cotylosaurs were members of the first group of reptiles. They looked like crocodiles and were the first to lay eggs.

Dimetrodon *(dye-met-ruh-don)*

Dimetrodon had jaws like reptiles and legs that were mammal-like.

Fingertip Facts *(cont.)*

Thecondont *(thee-kuhn-dont)*

Thecondonts were the dominant life form during the Triassic Period. They were reptiles and the ancestors of the dinosaurs.

Coelophysis *(see-lo-fiss-iss)*

Coelophysis the earliest known dinosaur. It was a small, hollow-boned creature with sharp claws and teeth.

Stegosaurus *(steg-uh-sawr-us)*

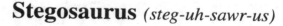

Ichthyosaur *(ik-thee-uh-sawr)*

Ichthyosaurs, snails, and jellyfish were plentiful in the oceans of the Triassic World.

Fingertip Facts *(cont.)*

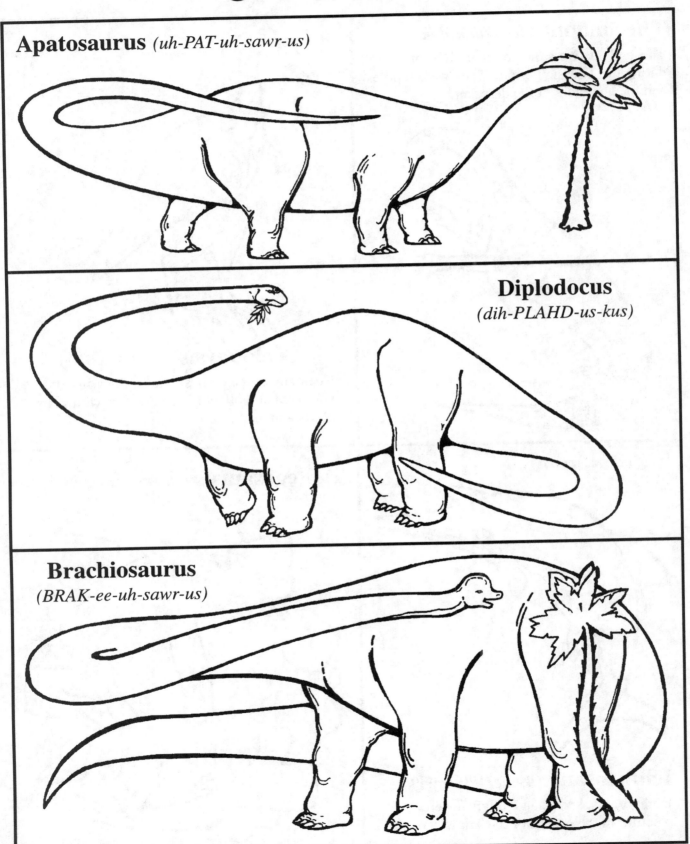

Apatosaurus *(uh-PAT-uh-sawr-us)*

Diplodocus
(dih-PLAHD-us-kus)

Brachiosaurus
(BRAK-ee-uh-sawr-us)

Fingertip Facts *(cont.)*

Ankylosaurus
(ang-KILE-us-sawr-us)

Allosaurus *(Al-uh-sawr-us)*

Corythosaurus
(ko-RITH-uh-sawr-us)

Iguanodon
(ig-WAN-oh-don)

Fingertip Facts *(cont.)*

Parasaurolophus
(par-ah-sawr-O-luh-fus)

Pachycephalosaurus
(pak-ee-SEF-uh-lo-sawr-us)

Triceratops
(try-SAIR-uh-tops)

Styracosaurus
(sty-RAK-uh-sawr-us)

Fingertip Facts *(cont.)*

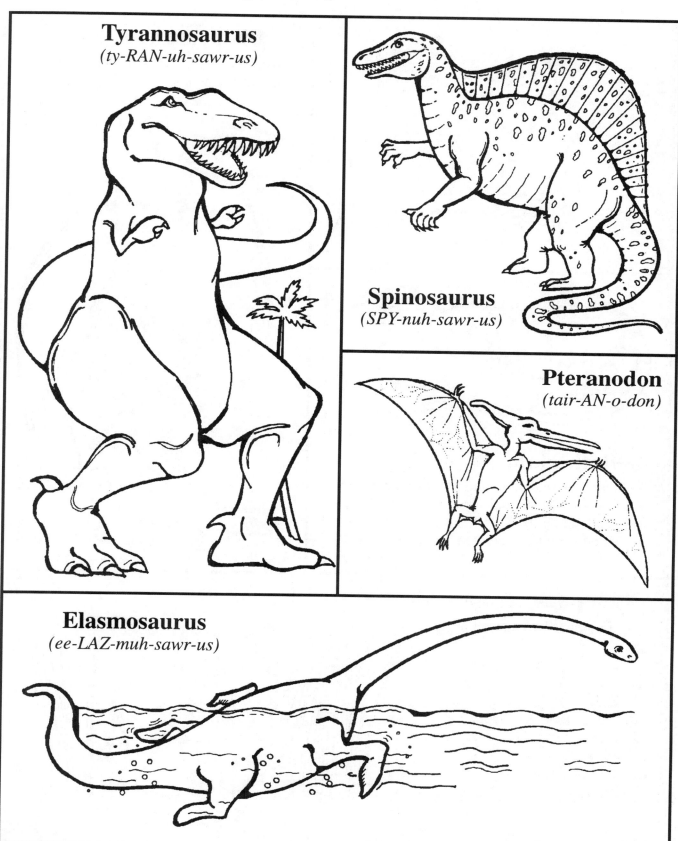

Tyrannosaurus
(ty-RAN-uh-sawr-us)

Spinosaurus
(SPY-nuh-sawr-us)

Pteranodon
(tair-AN-o-don)

Elasmosaurus
(ee-LAZ-muh-sawr-us)

Fingertip Facts *(cont.)*

Pterodactylus
(tair-uh-DAK-til-us)

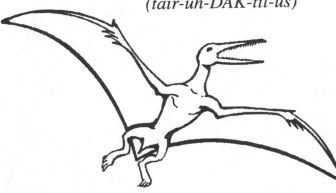

Diatryma *(di-uh-try-ma)*
Diatryma was a bird with sharp claws and furry feathers.

Deltatherium *(del-ta-theer-ee-um)*
Mammals increased in numbers during the late Cretaceous Period. One example was Deltatherium, a small rat-like mammal with a furry body and long, pointed snout.

Eohippus *(ee-uh-hip-pus)*
Eohippus was a small horse.

Fingertip Facts *(cont.)*

Wooly Mammoth
(wool-ee Mam-oth)

The wooly mammoth was covered in fur and had long, sharp tusks.

Smilodon *(smy-lo-don)*

A smilodon was a saber-tooth cat.

Fish

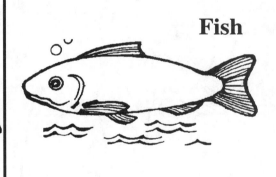

Bird

Glyptodon *(glip-toh-don)*

Glyptodon had armor covering and a spiked-club tail.

Fingertip Facts *(cont.)*

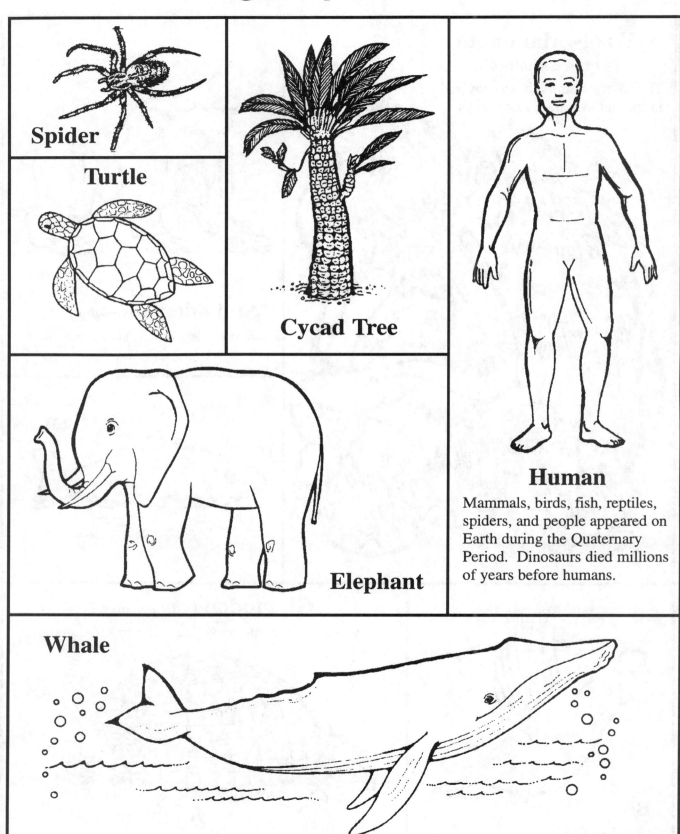

Spider

Turtle

Cycad Tree

Elephant

Human

Mammals, birds, fish, reptiles, spiders, and people appeared on Earth during the Quaternary Period. Dinosaurs died millions of years before humans.

Whale

76

Fingertip Facts *(cont.)*

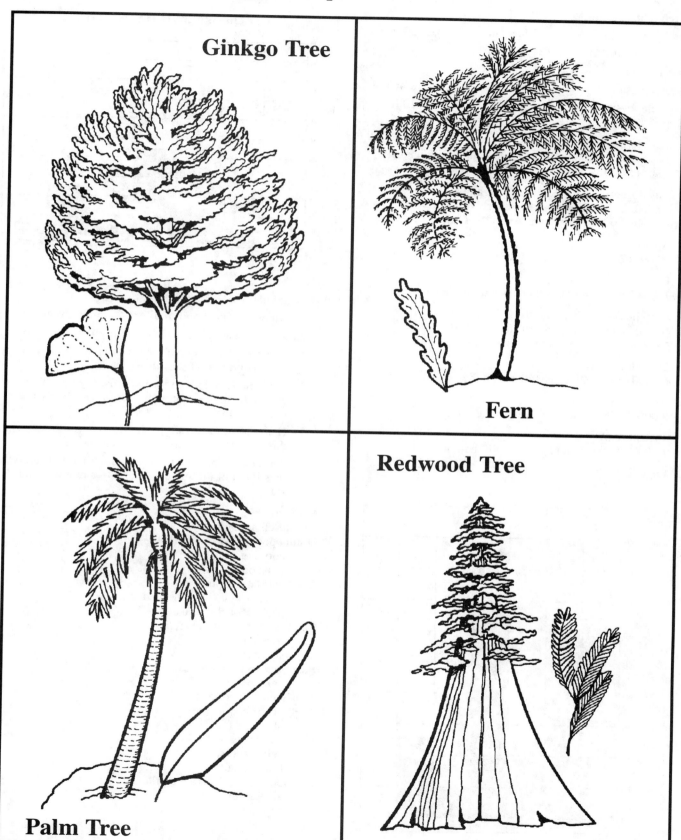

Ginkgo Tree

Fern

Palm Tree

Redwood Tree

Answer Key

Page 13

Height & Length

Tyrannosaurs	20 feet tall	50 feet long
Diplodocus	24 feet tall	90 feet long
Stegosaurus	16 feet tall	25 feet long
Brachiosaurus	44 feet tall	85 feet long
Coelophysis	4 feet tall	10 feet long
Triceratops	12 feet tall	25 feet long

Allosaurus, Spinosaurus &
Parasaurolophus|8,000x3=24,000 pounds all together
8,000+2,000=4 elephants weigh the same

Ankylosaurus, Iguanodon & Triceratops
10,000x2=20,000 pounds together
10,000+2,000=5 elephants weigh the same

Apatosaurus
60,000+2,000=30 elephants weigh the same

Brachiosaurus
160,000+2,000=80 elephants weigh the same

Corythosaurus, Stegosaurus & Styracosaurus
6,000x3=18,000 pounds together
6,000+2,000=3 elephants weigh the same

Diplodocus
50,000+2,000=25 elephants weigh the same

Pachycephalosaurus
2,000+2,000=1 elephant weighs the same

Tyrannosaurs
12,000+2,000=6 elephants weight the same

Page 14

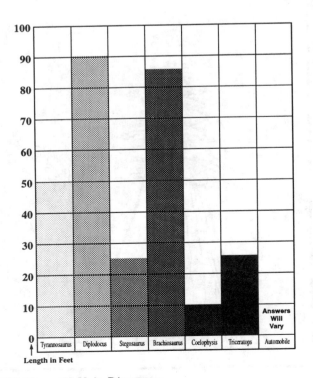

Page 15

Dinosaur Height Graph

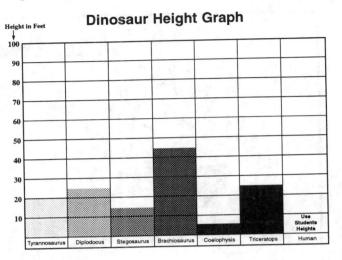

Page 24

How Fossils Are Formed

1. Dinosaurs lived on Earth for 160 million years.
2. All dinosaurs died suddenly 65 million years ago.
3. The bodies of some of the dinosaurs were covered by sand and dirt after they died.
4. The bones are hidden for millions of years. Water and minerals seep through the soil and slowly turn the bones to stone.
5. Heavy winds and rain wash away part of the sand and dirt, then a part of the dinosaur can be seen.
6. A scientist finds the fossil of a dinosaur and carefully digs it out of the stone to take it to a museum and study.

Page 27

Ornithischian Dinosaurs
Ornithopoda (bird-footed reptile)
    corythosaurus
    iguanodon
    parasaurolophus
Pachycephalosaur (thick-headed reptiles)
    pachycephalosaurus
Ceratopsia (horned-face reptile)
    triceratops
    styracosaurus
Stegosaur (plated reptiles)
    ankylosaurus
Saurischian Dinosaurs
Theropoda (beast-footed reptiles)
    allosaurus
    coelophysis
    spinosaurus
    tyrannosaurs
Sauropoda (lizard-footed reptiles)
    apatosaurus
    brachiosaurus
    diplodocus

Page 28

Ornithischian Dinosaurs

1. had hipbones shaped like those of a bird
2. were all plant eaters
3. has five subgroups
4. had hoofed toes
5. had beak-like mouths

Saurischian Dinosaurs

1. had hipbones shaped like those of a lizard
2. included plant and meat eaters
3. had clawed feet
4. has two subgroups

Both Groups

1. were both large and small
2. lived all over the world
3. lived during the Mesozoic Era

Page 39

Major Group	Subgroup	Name	Picture
vertebrate	Reptile	snake	
vertebrate	Bird	duck	
vertebrate	Fish	catfish	
vertebrate	Amphibian	frog	
vertebrate	Mammall	raccoon	
vertebrate	Dinosauria	protoceratops	
invertebrate	worm	earthworm	
invertebrate	Centipede/Millipede	thousand leg	
invertebrate	Insect	dragon fly	
invertebrate	Crustacean	lobster	
invertebrate	Snail	conch	
invertebrate	Spider	brown spider	

Page 40

Tyrannosaurs = tyrant lizard
Deinonycus = terrible claw
Allosaurus = different lizard
Brachiosaurus = arm lizard
Troodon = wounding teeth
Corythosaurus = helmet lizard
Diplodocus = double bean
Iguanodon = teeth like an iguana
Maiasaura = good mother lizard
Parasaurolophus = similar crested lizard
Ankylosaurus = stiffened lizard
Stegosaurus = covered or plated lizard
Coelophysis = hollow form
Styracosaurus = spiked lizard
Apatosaurus = deceptive lizard
Triceratops = three horned face
Velociraptor = swift robber

Page 43

1. cosmetic
2. polish
3. paint
4. film
5. gel
6. linoleum
7. rubber
8. iodine
9. soda
10. algin

Page 45

1. Ankylosaurus
2. Triceratops
3. Pachycephalosaurus
4. Stegosaurus
5. Tyrannosaurs
6. Apatosaurus

Page 50

1. Palozoic Era, Mesozoic Era, and Cenozoic Eta
2. Palozoic: began 600 million years ago, ended 225 million years ago

   Mesozoic: began 225 million years ago, ended 65 million years ago

   Cenozoic: began 65 million years ago, present time
3. Cenozoic Era; Quaternary Period
4. Cambrian Period
5. Mesozoic Era
6. Quaternary Period
7. No

Page 56

```
F A D I M E T R O D O N T A B
T R I C E R A T O P S B R B R
Y S P S P I N O S A U R U S S
R U L I T A P A U C D A A I A
A R O G E T N N R F E N S C C
N U D U R O K U A N K L O S
N A O A A U Y A G H Y S D H
O S C N K G L S P L U I S
S O U N O H I T O H U R P U
A C S D D J U L I L A S U R
U K O O I E S H M S A O A U
R T N N O M A C N O U S A S
U Y A Y C P G R A V M R R O L
S T E G O S A U R U S U T C L
Y S A O A F L A B W A S A E O
T S U T E X A T R X L Y P E L
D I N O S A U R S T E U A K
```

Bibliography

Fiction

Adler, David A. *The Dinosaur Princess and Other Prehistoric Riddles.* Holiday, 1988.

Bonham, Frank. *The Friends of the Loony Lake Monster.* Dutton, 1972.

Butterworth, Oliver. *The Enormous Egg.* Little, Brown & Co., 1956.

Cole, Joanna. *The Magic School Bus® in the Time of the Dinosaurs.* Scholastic, 1994.

Crichton, Michael. Adapted by Mike Teitelbaum. *Welcome to Jurassic Park.* Western Publishing Company, 1993.

Gurney, James. *Dinotopia.* Turner Publishing, Inc., 1992.

Rogers, Jean. *Dinosaurs Are 568.* Greenwillow, 1988.

Steme, Noelle. *Tyrannosaurs Wrecks: A Book of Dinosaur Riddles.* Harper, 1979.

Nonfiction

Arnold, Caroline. *Dinosaurs All Around: An Artist's View of the Prehistoric World.* Clarion, 1993.

Booth, Jerry. *The Big Beast Book: Dinosaurs and How They Got That Way.* Little, Brown & Co., 1988.

Cobb, Vicki. *The Monsters Who Died: A Mystery About Dinosaurs.* Putnam, 1983.

Dixon, Dougal. *Dinosaurs, The Fossil Hunters.* Highlights for Children, 1993.

Lagneau, Nicole. *The Life of Prehistoric Animals.* Macdonald Educational Limited, 1976.

Poetry

Prelutsky, Jack. *Something Big Has Been Here.* William Morrow, 1990.

Prelutsky, Jack. *Tyrannosaurs Was a Beast.* Scholastic, 1988.

Silverstein, Shel. *A Light in the Attic.* Harper & Row, 1981.

Silverstein, Shel. *Where the Sidewalk Ends.* Harper & Row, 1974.

Reference

Microsoft Encarta96 Encyclopedia. Microsoft Corporation, 1996.

Richardson, James. *Science Dictionary of Dinosaurs.* RGA Publishing Group, 1992.

Sattler, Helen Roney. *The Illustrated Dinosaur Dictionary.* William Morrow, 1983.

Wexo, John Bonnett. *Prehistoric Zoobooks: Volumes One - Ten.* Wildlife Education, Ltd., 3590 Kettner Blvd, San Diego, CA 92101

World Book Encyclopedia. Field Enterprises Educational Corporation, 1988.

Children's Books on Dinosaurs and Related Concepts

Brandenberg, Aliki. *Digging Up Dinosaurs.* Harper & Row, 1985.

Brandenberg, Aliki. *My Visit to the Dinosaurs.* Harper & Row, 1985.

Clark, Mary Lou. *Dinosaurs, A New True Book.* Regensteiner Publishing Enterprises, Inc., 1981.

Eastman, David. *Prehistoric Animals.* Troll Associates, 1977.

Joyce, William. *Dinosaur Bob and His Adventures with the Family* Lazardo. Scholastic, 1988.

Most, Bernard. *Whatever Happened to the Dinosaurs?* Harcourt Brace & Company, 1984.

Needham, Kate. *The Time Trekkers Visit the Dinosaurs.* Aladdin Books Ltd., 1995.

Nolan, Dennis. *Dinosaur Dream.* Trumpet Club, 1990.

Parish, Peggy. *Dinosaur Time.* Scholastic, 1974.

Rowe, Erna. *Giant Dinosaurs.* Scholastic, 1975.

Watson, Jane Werner. *Dinosaurs.* Western Publishing, 1959.